THE IMITATION OF CHRIST

Miss Betty I. Knott, who translated this book, is Lecturer in Comparative Philology in the Department of Humanity, Glasgow University.

THE IMITATION
OF CHRIST

by
Thomas à Kempis

Translated by
Betty I. Knott

Collins
FOUNT PAPERBACKS

First published in Fontana Books 1963
Reprinted in Fount Paperbacks January 1977
Fifteenth Impression October 1982

© *in the introduction, Betty I. Knott, 1963*
© *in translation Wm. Collins Sons & Co. Ltd, 1963*

Made and printed in Great Britain by
William Collins Sons & Co. Ltd, Glasgow

*The quotations from the Bible in this book are from the
translation by Monsignor R. A. Knox, and are included by
kind permission of his Eminence the Cardinal Archbishop
of Westminster and of Messrs. Burns and Oates Ltd.*

CONTENTS

BOOK 2 : SOME ADVICE ON THE INNER LIFE

BOOK 3: SPIRITUAL COMFORT

BOOK 4: A REVERENT RECOMMENDATION TO HOLY COMMUNION

INTRODUCTION

1. *Thomas à Kempis and the Brethren of the Common Life*

The appearance of *The Imitation of Christ* in the earlier part of the fifteenth century is no isolated phenomenon, but only one manifestation of a widespread devotional movement that occurred in the fourteenth and fifteenth centuries. Whatever may have been the reasons (and many have been suggested), this period is characterized by an increased concern for personal experience in religion, for vitality and reality in the inner life of the spirit, achieved through the practice of private prayer, meditation and self-discipline. Such a spirit had always been present in the Church, and had flourished especially within the religious orders, but at certain periods it was more intense and more generally manifested than at others. This is the case in the period under consideration. At this time there was a revival of the devotional spirit not only in the monasteries, but among those members of the Church who spent their lives in the world, among clergy[1] and lay-people, among educated and uneducated. Its effect in individual lives ranged from simple piety to the deepest experiences of mysticism, as we see from the considerable body of devotional and mystical literature produced at this time.[2]

[1] The term ' clergy ' or ' clerks ' meant primarily men in orders in distinction to laymen. Orders could be major (those of deacon, priest, bishop), or minor (e.g. acolytes). Minor orders, which were often taken by young students, did not involve celibacy or necessarily presuppose progression to major orders.

[2] For example, in France the writings of John Gerson (1363-1429); in Italy, Catherine of Siena (1347-80); in Germany and the Netherlands, Meister Eckhart (1260-1327),

Compared with previous devotional movements, the fourteenth-century movement is remarkable for its popular character, and consequently it found in many places a practical rather than a speculative outlet. This was so in the Netherlands and the Rhineland, where it was particularly strong, and where it manifested itself in the establishment of small communities, chiefly of lay-people, who spontaneously banded themselves together with the express purpose of providing in the world a setting for the practice of personal religion and attainment of knowledge of God. One of the most important and influential of these organizations was that which went by the name of Brethren of the Common Life.

The writer of *The Imitation of Christ,* Thomas à Kempis, was, between the ages of thirteen and twenty, linked with the members of this organization through the ties of gratitude, friendship and admiration, and it is clear from his own writings that we must look to them for the influences that set the pattern of his spiritual life. *The Imitation of Christ* and the other devotional writings of Thomas à Kempis emerge from a background in which the Brethren of the Common Life are the most important figures. It is his association with these people that not only connects him with the devotional movement of the whole period but is responsible in large measure for his personal expression of it.

The Brethren of the Common Life owed their existence to two men in particular, Gerhard Groote (1340-84) and Florentius Radewijns (1350-1400). These were men of education, Groote being a Master of Arts of Paris, Florentius of Prague, and both were in orders.

Henry Suso (1295-1366), John Tauler (1300-61), John Ruysbroeck (1293-1381); in England, Walter Hilton (d. 1396), Julian of Norwich (1342—after 1413), Margery Kempe (1373 —after 1433).

Groote taught for a time at Cologne, enjoying the income from a canonry at Aix and several other benefices besides. He was also a rich man in his own right, the son of an influential family in Deventer, and at first he lived in the comfort that would be expected of a man in his position. He was, however, converted through a Carthusian prior to a desire for a more spiritual and ascetic form of life, and soon afterwards renounced all his benefices and most of his worldly possessions, keeping only enough to supply his essential needs. Although he retired for three years to a Carthusian monastery, he was dissuaded from taking religious vows as it was felt that his talents could be more profitably employed in a different calling. Instead he took deacon's orders, which entitled him to preach, and embarked on an extensive and successful mission in the Netherlands, attacking abuses in the Church and urging the crowds who came to hear him to repent of their worldliness and indifference to spiritual things. This roused such opposition in some quarters that in 1383 he was forbidden to preach; whereupon he retired to his house in the town of Deventer, and lived there very quietly and simply, devoting himself to study and prayer and becoming well known for his holiness and good works.

His sermons and personal example were not without effect, however, for many people from all classes were moved to adopt in the setting of their own homes and normal daily lives the simple prayerful way of life which he advocated. The motivating force of this way of life was to be found in *devotio*, ' devotion ' or ' love for God ',[3] and so essential was this characteristic that

---

[3] ' Devotion ' is a reverent and loving desire for God that finds its expression in wholehearted dedication to his service. It is both the will to serve him and the inward desires and joys experienced in that service. It is ' a will to give oneself readily to the things that pertain to the service of God ' (St Thomas Aquinas, S.T. II, II, 82. 1); ' devotion is simply the

those who thus followed Groote's example adopted or acquired the name *devoti*, 'the Devout', and the whole movement towards dedication and piety among lay-people that Groote thus originated came to be known as Devotio Moderna, 'the New [or contemporary] Devotion'.

All walks of life were represented among Groote's converts, but some of his closest followers were a group of young clerks for whom Groote's scholarly interests and reputation were a special attraction. Among these was Florentius, one of the clergy attached to the cathedral in Deventer. The adherence of these educated men meant that the Devotio Moderna was from the start further characterized by an insistence on the value of good learning and the importance of reading for growth in understanding and sound development in the inner life.

In pursuance of his ideal of a life of poverty, Groote had given up most of his large house to a group of devout women who lived there together, though without any vows or rigid organization, giving most of their time to prayer, meditation and charitable works. Such associations of devout lay-women were at that time not uncommon. Florentius now took into his own house a number of the young clerks who were closely associated with Groote, and there they set up a form of communal life. A number of like-minded laymen joined them. Eventually these young men expressed a desire that the way of life they had adopted should be recognized as a life in common and be formally established. Groote had some doubts about the wisdom of creating such an unofficial group outside the organization of the Church, but eventually he gave his consent and the

---

ardent longing of the soul for God' (Florentius); it is 'the prosecution of the journey *to* God and *in* God' (E. Underhill, *Mysticism*, p. 130). Devotion is one of the essential concepts of the *Imitation of Christ*.

community adopted the name of Brethren of the Common Life.

Though the impulse to this whole devotional movement came from Groote, it was thus Florentius's name that was connected with the actual establishment of the first group of Brethren, and his house was venerated by later groups both in Deventer and elsewhere as the original home of the organization. For the fame of this community soon spread abroad, and devout people in neighbouring towns (e.g. Zwolle and Amersfoort) began to form similar associations of their own. Subsequent foundations followed the pattern of the first group, and the houses of Brethren usually consisted, as the first group did, of clerks and lay-people, with one or two priests. Similar associations of women were also formed, and before long communities of Brethren and Sisters of the Common Life were in existence in many towns of the Netherlands.

We are fairly well informed as to the way of life in the original community of Brethren on which the others were modelled. Less is known of the detailed organization of the groups of women, but the same general principles directed their communities as those of the men.

We are told that the intention of the first Brethren was to create a Christian community as they imagined it to have existed in New Testament times. The members of the group were not asked to commit themselves for any definite period or to take any vows, but on entering the community they undertook to give up their independence and to live under the direction of the rector, contributing all their personal resources to the common fund. At long as they remained members of the household they were expected to conform to the ideals of poverty, chastity and obedience. The living was frugal, as many of the members were poor and a great deal was given away to the needy, and while no special habit was worn, clothes were expected to be plain and serviceable, and any refinement in dress or personal possessions was discouraged. All were to be serious-minded, not given to unnecessary laughter and talking, and meals were taken in silence, listening to a reading from the Bible or some devotional book. Much time was set aside for the reading of religious and devotional literature, and for meditation and prayer with regular attendance at Church services. One of the most marked features of the community life was the regular practice of discussing together personal spiritual problems, and this was intended to foster fellowship, charity and humility.

The Brethren were, however, decidedly active as well as contemplative. In the first place, great importance was attached to manual labour, and every member, whether clerk or lay, had to contribute by physical activity to the maintenance of the group. For laymen this usually meant household tasks such as cooking, sewing, etc. For the educated it was the hard work of preparing and copying by hand, books which could be sold. In this insistence on manual labour the Brethren were following the example of the various religious orders whose Rule expressly enjoined physical activity of some kind on the monks. At the same time the Brethren were seeking to avoid any suspicion of heresy, such as attached to certain lay communities of doubtful beliefs which devoted themselves to the contemplative life and supported themselves by begging.

The active life further manifested itself in practical assistance of those in need, and the Brethren performed many unobtrusive good works in the way of feeding and clothing the poor. They also cared for the spiritual needs of those around them by preaching (if qualified to do so), by teaching, and by providing, through their activities as copyists, devotional books in Dutch and German such as could be read by lay-people.

In particular they took an interest in the boys attending the schools of the area. In the late fourteenth century the schools of the Netherlands had a considerable fame, and boys came from some distance to attend them. As many of them were poor, they were largely dependent on charity for board, lodging, books and other equipment, and their inexperience meant that they were often in need of guidance and advice. Groote and Florentius had a natural connection with the schools of Zwolle and Deventer through their friendship with the rectors John Cele and John Boeme, who were men of the same outlook as themselves, and the Brethren did much to help the boys studying there. They cared for their material needs by helping them to find suitable lodgings, and eventually they acquired a hostel close to the House of the Brethren for them to live in (an institution which became a regular feature of later communities of Brethren). Scholars who showed any skill in writing they trained as copyists to help in supplying the growing demand for devotional literature, an occupation which at the same time provided some of the money required for school fees, etc.

But the chief concern of the Brethren was for the mental and spiritual development of the scholars. For this reason they were encouraged, like other members of the general public, to associate with the Brethren at certain times in the week when Florentius's house was opened to visitors for the purpose of hearing sermons and sharing in discussions on the inner life. In this way many of the young students early became acquainted with the Brethren and their ideals, and they developed an enthusiasm for the religious life which later led them to join a community of Brethren and eventually to enter a monastery. Such a monastery was very often a house of Austin canons, for the Brethren developed a very close association and especial relationship with this order through the action of Groote.

The anomalous organization of the Brethren, bearing
many resemblances to the life of a regular community
yet made up of people living in the world and not
bound by vows, began to arouse considerable opposition, especially among the Friars. This, combined
with the fact that many of his followers wished for the
full religious life, made it increasingly imperative that
Groote should realize a desire he had long cherished,
and found a house of religious belonging to one of the
established orders, namely that of the regular Austin
canons.[4] His choice of this order was due to a large
extent to his association with John Ruysbroeck, the
Flemish mystic and first prior of the Austin canons at
Groenendael. Groote had a great respect for Ruysbroeck, both personally and as religious teacher, and
had visited him at Groenendael together with John
Cele. From him he had received advice and support
in his missionary activities, and when he conceived the
idea of founding a house of religious himself, it was
Ruysbroeck's community that he took as his ideal.

He was prevented from putting his plans into effect
by his death in 1384, but others carried out his wishes.
By 1387 it was possible for a small group of Groote's
followers who had become Brethren to be formally
constituted as a house of Austin canons at Windesheim.
Other foundations soon followed. The monastery at
Mount St Agnes near Zwolle dates from 1398. Later
convents of canonesses of the same order were established, and by 1496 Windesheim was the mother-house
of about one hundred foundations, including twenty
nunneries. The communities of Brethren and Sisters

---

[4] These were clerks who lived a communal life of poverty,
chastity and obedience according to the rule of St Augustine.
They differed from monks in that they were less strictly
enclosed and could undertake the responsibility of a parish
or other duties which required their presence outside the
walls of their house, but they did not necessarily do so. The
order came into being at the end of the eleventh century.

in the towns did not go out of existence with this expansion of the regular communities, but continued for some time to flourish and increase throughout Holland, Belgium and Germany, and at first it remained customary to enter the monasteries of the order by way of the secular communities. The greatest harmony existed between the two groups, which were conscious of their common descent, and looked back to Groote as the inspirer of their way of life, calling him ' the founder of our devotion '. In both, the traditions of the original Brethren were preserved, with emphasis on sound learning, manual labour, and devotion nourished by contemplation and prayer.

It was in these circles that Thomas à Kempis spent almost the whole of his long life.

He was born in the year 1379 or 1380 to John and Gertrude Haemerken of Kempen, a small town about forty miles from Cologne. There was also an older son John, born in 1365. Although their parents were far from wealthy, both boys went to Deventer to attend the school there like many others from the Rhineland. It was partly because of Groote's presence in the area that students were drawn from so far afield, and many of these were attracted into the Devotio Moderna. John à Kempis became one of Groote's pupils and followers, and subsequently played quite a considerable part in the establishment of the monastic branch of the movement. He was one of the first six to take the habit in the new foundation of Austin canons at Windesheim, and on the founding of the monastery at Mount St Agnes he was transferred from Windesheim to become its first prior.

When Thomas in turn arrived at Deventer about 1392, he was advised by his brother to apply for help and guidance to Florentius, who was by this time not only rector of the organized community of Brethren in that town but leader of the whole movement in succession to Groote. Thomas tells how Florentius showed him particular kindness throughout the seven or eight years of his stay in Deventer, helping him materially and spiritually, and for a year receiving him into the community of young clerks associated with the Brethren. During this time he became acquainted with many of the first generation of Groote's followers and had ample opportunity for observing their practices and listening to their discussions on the spiritual life. It was the custom of the *devoti* to make collections of sayings on spiritual topics, and Thomas followed this practice, noting down from the conversations of Florentius and other devout members of the household much teaching on the inward life and practical advice on growth in devotion that eventually he incorporated into his own devotional works.

Years later he wrote lives of Florentius and his followers for the edification of novices (and also of Groote, though he never knew him personally). He writes of them all with affection and respect, but it was Florentius above all others who won his love and admiration. The biography is full of personal memories that record the profound impression made upon him by Florentius's generosity, self-discipline, humility and devotion.

Eventually Thomas too felt a desire to become a religious, and in 1399, on the advice of Florentius, he entered the house where his brother was prior. As it was not permitted for blood brothers to be full members of the same religious community, he remained for six years a *donatus* (a kind of lay brother), but when John à Kempis was due to be transferred elsewhere he was in 1406 accepted as a novice and soon received the habit.

Of the remainder of his life we have only a bare outline. In 1413 he was ordained priest; some time after this he was elected sub-prior, and held that office during the troubled years 1429-32, when there were disturbances over the election to the see of Utrecht, and the canons of St Agnes were forced to leave their house and go into exile in Frisia. Some time after their return we find Thomas as steward, but an early account of his life records that he was relieved of this office, which was uncongenial to one of his devout and unworldly nature. Later he was appointed novice-master, and in 1448 he again held the office of sub-prior.

Amidst all these duties he found time not only to copy a considerable number of manuscripts but also to write many works of his own. Some of these were the outcome of his conscientious tenure of the various offices—e.g. *The Faithful Steward, Sermons to Novices,* and *Dialogues with Novices*. Besides these, there were other sermons *To the Brothers* and *On the Life and Passion of the Lord*; there were prayers, poems, books on the monastic life—*The Discipline of the Religious, The Life of the Good Monk*—and meditations on many subjects : *The Soliloquy of the Soul, The Garden of Roses, The Valley of Lilies, On True Compunction of Heart, A Meditation on the Incarnation of Christ,* etc. There were historical writings as well, including a chronicle of the monastery which he continued faithfully up to his death in his ninety-second year in 1471.

The writer who continued the chronicle after Thomas's death records that his fellows remembered him as one who had seen the difficult early years of Mount St Agnes, and who had contributed to the building up of the place materially and spiritually by his own writings and by the copies he made, in the tradition of the early Brethren, of many books, including the complete Bible used by the monastery. They also thought of him as a man of devotion and kindness, 'filled with love for the Passion of the Lord, and a wonderful comforter of those in temptation and trouble '.[5]

II. *The Imitation of Christ*

The Imitation of Christ is the best known of the many works attributed to Thomas à Kempis, and one which has been read and valued continually since the time of its first publication. It was written during the earlier part of the fifteenth century (all the books being known by 1427), and the fame and popularity it soon won throughout Western Europe are attested by the number of manuscript copies extant, by the translations that were very soon made into Dutch, German, French, English and Italian, and by the printed editions that were produced towards the end of the century.

The four books of which it is traditionally composed were originally four separate treatises, not designed as a whole by their author nor written at one time. Because of their popularity, however, they were included more often than any others in selections from the devotional writings of Thomas, and their similarity of theme and inspiration made it natural for copyists to transcribe them together. In this way various combinations and arrangements of the booklets appeared, but the one that proved most successful was a version in four books which was the first to be printed and remains the one best known today.

The title *De Imitatione Christi* (*Concerning the Imitation of Christ*) by which the work was usually known belonged in the first place to Book 1 only. It is nothing more in origin than the first words of that book (or more precisely of the heading summarizing the contents of the first chapter) which it was customary to cite for reference purposes—e.g. ' here begins the treatise " con-

[5] Chronicle of Mount St Agnes, ch. 30.

cerning the imitation of Christ".' These words soon
acquired the force of a title, and when it became
normal practice to treat the four books as parts of one
work and to publish them together in the order that is
now familiar, this title was extended to cover the whole
volume, replacing the separate headings given to the
four books by the author.[6] Some other titles are known
—one version of the work containing only three of the
books was entitled *Musica Ecclesiastica*—but it was *De
Imitatione Christi* that won general acceptance.

The traditional attribution of the work to Thomas à
Kempis is by no means uncontested. At various times
it has been ascribed to thirty-five different people—
including Groote, Walter Hilton the English mystic,
Suso, Tauler, John Gersen Abbot of Vercelli, St Bernard, Bonaventura, Innocent III, and John Gerson,
Chancellor of the University of Paris. Considerable
controversy has raged over the identity of the writer,
particularly in the seventeenth and nineteenth centuries.
The chief supporters of the various theories were often
not a little influenced by the desire to claim the writer
for their own country or their own religious order.

The source of the controversy lies in the fact that
the *Imitation,* like many other devotional works at the
time, was published anonymously. It was in the first
place written and transcribed for the members of the
communities attached to the mother-house of Windesheim, and in such circles the name of the author would
be well known. It was only as the *Imitation* achieved
its immensely wide circulation outside this group of

[6] The printed edition of 1471 introduces the work in the
following way: 'Here begins a book of consolation for the
instruction of the devout, the first chapter of which deals with
the imitation of Christ and contempt for the worthless things
of the world. Some people call the whole book *The Imitation
of Christ,* just as the Gospel according to St Matthew is called
The Book of the Generation of Jesus Christ, because the first
chapter speaks of the generation of Christ according to the
flesh.'

monastic houses and among the general public that the
possibility of wrong attribution arose.

It is not merely a question of anonymity, however.
Much of the controversy since as early as the seventeenth century has centred round the manuscript copy
of the *Imitation* made by Thomas à Kempis himself in
1441. This particular copy[7] (which is not the only one
in existence from the hand of Thomas), contains the
books of the *Imitation* in the order 1, 2, 4, 3, together
with a selection of other works of which he is generally
held to have been the author. It concludes with the
following words: 'finished and completed in the year
of our Lord 1441 by the hand of Brother Thomas à
Kempis at Mount St Agnes near Zwolle'. Thomas
here states that he has copied out the works in the
manuscript, but makes no claim to authorship, and
this omission has been emphasized by those who believe
on other grounds that Thomas à Kempis did not write
this work. Of itself such a statement neither proves nor
disproves authorship. Thomas was at this point making
a copy of writings at least some of which had first been
published many years before, and there was no reason
why, if he were the author, he should choose to assert
this fact now if he had not done so originally—especially
as this particular copy seems to have been intended for
his own community, with whom it remained until 1577.
There may have been special reasons which we can now
only guess at that led him to give this manuscript his
seal of authenticity by stating that he had copied it
himself, but it is simplest to assume that he was con-
forming to the common practice of copyists in adding
his name at the end, particularly if it marked the completion of a task which had taken some years.

Of the many people to whom the *Imitation* has been
attributed at various times, the most serious rival to
Thomas à Kempis and the one whose claims have been

[7] Now in the Royal Library in Brussels.

upheld most persistently is John Gerson, Chancellor of
Paris. He was contemporary with Thomas, a well-
known figure in ecclesiastical affairs, and a writer of a
number of devotional works. The claims of Gerson rest
largely on the number and the early date of the editions
which assign the *Imitation* to him, and there is no
doubt that this evidence cannot be dismissed lightly.
The details of the manuscript tradition of the *Imitation*
are complicated, and accounts of the relationship and
date of the various copies are far from unanimous. It
seems, however, that there may be as many as twenty-
eight attributions of the *Imitation* to Gerson from the
fifteenth century (either in manuscript or in printed
editions), some of which belong to the lifetime of
Thomas himself—the first clear dated attribution to
Gerson occurring in a manuscript copy of 1460.

It is not difficult to explain how an anonymous and
widely-read work such as the *Imitation* came to be
attributed to a well-known figure like Gerson. Apart
from the fact that his name was familiar, Gerson's
devotional works drew their inspiration to some extent
from the same sources that contributed to the New
Devotion, and they were read and copied fairly exten-
sively by the Windesheim communities. Treatises
written by Thomas were frequently issued in the same
volume as selections from the writings of Gerson, just
as they were combined with those of other writers.
Many of the early attributions to Gerson occur in
editions produced in France, and the immediate
source of this development may lie in a volume which
appeared in 1462 containing a French translation of
Book 3 of the *Imitation* together with a number of
Gerson's sermons.

Against Gerson's authorship may be quoted the fact
that none of the books of the *Imitation* appear in the
list of Gerson's works compiled by his brother in 1423,
nor in the first printed edition of his works issued in

1483. Also, Gerson was not a monk, and it seems a reasonable supposition that the author of the *Imitation* was. As regards contents and style, some have found similarities between the *Imitation* and writings of Gerson, others have said that the style is utterly dissimilar and the whole temper of the work alien to the theologian who took such an active part in the councils of the Church at this period.

On the other side there are the many early manuscripts and editions which definitely ascribe the work to Thomas, and some of these expressly reject the claims of Gerson at the same time. Thirteen manuscripts dated before 1500 name Thomas as the author, the earliest one (in Brussels) dated 1425. At least twelve printed editions of the fifteenth century attribute the work to Thomas, including the earliest, which appeared at Augsburg in 1471.

There are also the statements of contemporaries who had the chance of knowing Thomas personally. Among others, John Busch (1388-c. 1480), the historian of the community at Windesheim, speaks of 'Brother Thomas à Kempis, a man of proved goodness, the author of several devotional booklets including the one on the imitation of Christ which begins "He who follows me"'.[8]

There is also internal evidence from the *Imitation* itself. While making allowance for maturity of experience and development of style, one can readily discover similarities not only in subject matter, but in sentiment, association of ideas, and in phraseology, which link the *Imitation* with devotional treatises such as *The Soliloquy of the Soul, The Garden of Roses, The Valley of Lilies,* which are generally acknowledged as the work of Thomas à Kempis.

A second point is that the *Imitation* is so pervaded

[8] Chronicle of Windesheim, ch. 21. This work was written between 1456 and 1464.

by the ideals and beliefs of the Brethren of the Common Life that it is reasonable to look for its author in one who was as closely associated with that group as we know Thomas to have been. The similarity, for example, between the *Imitation* and the recorded sayings of Groote and Florentius that Thomas attached to his account of their lives shows how much the work owes to the inspiration of those spiritual leaders. On the other hand, while this similarity argues against Gerson, it has been made a basis for assigning the *Imitation* to Groote himself, or for seeing in Thomas à Kempis nothing more than a gifted editor who in this work gave the shape that is now familiar to Groote's essential teaching.

Though argument is today less violent, the matter has not been definitely settled. Considerable support is found for both Gerson and Groote, but opinion is mostly on the side of Thomas à Kempis.

The contents of the books in the order which is now usual may be summarized as follows:

In Book 1 the author is writing of the problems and temptations to be encountered in the first stages of the devotional life. (Book 1 contains more than the other three that relates directly to the monastic life, and it is thought that this book, which was the first to be published, was perhaps composed soon after Thomas's entry into the monastery, and that he is consciously adapting what he has to say to his audience of monks.) The earlier part of the book deals with the *separation* necessary for any who seek to follow Christ wholeheartedly, in particular separation from worldly knowledge and secular learning. This must be replaced by a humble desire for knowledge of God, which can only be achieved by self-knowledge and self-abhorrence. Such an attitude depends on utterly rejecting every interest external to the spirit, and concentrating on the life within. To attain complete freedom from the world the old desires must be put to death, and independence of external circumstances acquired by the curbing of natural instincts and emotions—for which the life of the community provides much opportunity. Only by freeing himself from all that could distract him can a man wholeheartedly seek God, and this means learning to dispense with the company of other people with all its possibilities of idle gossip and of filling the mind with extraneous thoughts. He must learn to keep to himself and to seek the company of God. Such a concentration is essential, for ' it does not take long for empty pursuits to defile and capture us again.' (ch. x)

Once such a course has been undertaken, progress in the spiritual life cannot be made without an effort of the will. The follower of Christ must set himself to resist sin and must consciously adopt an attitude of continual watchfulness and self-examination. As a result he becomes more aware of his sin and of its gravity. He is filled with loathing for it, and for the circumstances of this life that make him so subject to it; for all his struggles he comes to realize that he can never escape from sin while in this world. In fact earthly life seems to him nothing but a time of sorrow and distress and distraction from the things of the spirit.[9] Yet at the same time he learns the value of

[9] There is more emphasis in Book 1 than elsewhere in the *Imitation* on this consciousness of sin. It is here (especially ch. 21) that Thomas writes of the state of ' compunction of heart ', (v. Rayner Storr, *De Imitatione Christi: Concordance, s.v. compunctio*). ' Compunction of heart ' is ' a humbling of the mind combined with tears occasioned by the memory of sin and the fear of judgment '. It involves ' a realization of man's pilgrim state throughout the long years of this life, together with a yearning for the heavenly country ' (Isidore *Sent.* 2.12). Consequently it is more than repentance for specific sins. It is an awareness of one's guilty nature and general tendency to sin, which induces a habitual attitude of sorrow for the past and watchfulness for the future. Fear of judgment is not its only cause, but also love and desire for God, and unwillingness to grieve him.

adversity and discovers that the trials of this life provide a training-ground where the spirit is disciplined and enabled to make progress.

The qualities Thomas considers essential to develop are summarized in chapter 23—' an utter disregard of the world, a fervent desire for progress in virtue, a love of discipline, the practice of penitence, readiness to obey, denial of self, and acceptance of any adversity for the love of Christ '. The feeling of the book is one of challenge, of personal effort, of striving and toiling, and it is on this note that the book ends : ' your progress will depend on the roughness you show your old nature.'

The mood of Book 2 is quieter. While the difficulties of Book 1 still have to be faced, Thomas here emphasizes the refuge in the inner life where peace and quietness do not depend on external events. His gaze is turned inwards, and he knows that if a man seeks only God and his approval, he can submit calmly and humbly to all that life inflicts upon him. The secret of such a life lies in the friendship and fellowship of Christ. It is from Christ that we receive the grace we need if we are to live in this spirit, and his presence is the only true and real joy in this earthly life. Grace and humility are more prominent in this book than in Book 1. The author has learnt to rely less on his own efforts, and to rest quietly in the indwelling presence of Christ. It is to the inward joy of fellowship with Christ that Thomas returns again and again in this book, and it is significant that here more often than anywhere else he uses the name Jesus, the human name of Christ.

But this fellowship cannot be attained without sacrifice on our part. Sin and worldliness can soon drive Jesus away, so we must school ourselves to accepting the hardship of the way of the cross to which all followers of Christ are called. We must expect the pain of self-denial and the discomfort of discipline; we must

face the fact that suffering is an inevitable part of the
Christian life. The cross looms ever larger in the later
part of the book, and the last chapter ' on the royal way
of the holy cross' is framed at the beginning and end
with the command to renounce self, take up the cross
and follow Jesus. Yet it is in the later part of the book
also that the idea of spiritual comfort appears most
frequently, thus reiterating that spiritual joy cannot be
experienced without the pain of the cross.

Book 3 is entitled ' Spiritual Comfort ', and Thomas's
theme is once again the inward joy that comes from
fellowship with Christ. But this fellowship is not quite
that of Book 2. The Jesus of that book is here ' Domin-
us ', the Lord, and the believer is his humble disciple.
The spirit of this book is one of humility, of self-efface-
ment, of acknowledgment of the power of God and
acceptance of his will in all things. The disciple has no
eyes for any but his Lord, and he disciplines himself
in response to his commands.

Yet as he sees his own nothingness, he sees even
more clearly the love of the Lord who cares for him in
spite of his unworthiness, who looks on his natural
weakness and mercifully sends the all-powerful grace
that he needs so desperately and can never deserve. Yet
as he meditates on the love of his Lord and the wonders
of his grace, he feels the inadequacy of his own love;
he knows he does not yet feel the all-absorbing love that
overrides all obstacles and finds nothing hard. But the
glimpses he has, tell him that when a love like that is
experienced, anything a man is asked to suffer in this
life for the sake of Christ fades into insignificance; then
the whole of this world ceases to matter in the light of
the eternal kingdom to which the disciple longs to pass,
so that he can be with his Lord for ever.

The relation between the Lord and his disciple is a
particularly close one here, and this is reflected in the
dialogue form in which Thomas has cast the book.

Christ and the soul are pictured conversing together
in that quiet place where no one else may enter.

Book 4 is more obviously a unity than any of the
others. Its theme is the Sacrament of Holy Communion
and every chapter deals directly with some aspect of
this subject, whereas in the other books the author
allows himself to range over a much less restricted and
unified field. In the course of Book 4, Thomas has occasion to write of the responsibilities and feelings of the
priest as he consecrates and administers the Sacrament
(v. especially chs. v and xi). It is therefore assumed
that this book was written soon after Thomas's ordina-
tion to the priesthood in 1413, and earlier than Book
3 (and possibly than 2 also).

When he thinks of the Sacrament, Thomas thinks also
of *devotion*, that love for Christ that should fill the
believer whether he is receiving the Sacrament or meditating on it. The bond of love between the Lord and
his disciple which plays such an important part elsewhere is thus in Book 4 the constant theme. Once
again the Lord is speaking with his disciple, but now the
Lord is 'Dilectus', the Beloved, and through the Sacrament he comes as a divine guest to the house his disciple
prepares for him.

The disciple is aware of his unworthiness to receive
such a guest, yet he knows that he must receive him.
The Sacrament is essential, for 'it is the health of soul
and body, the remedy for every sickness of the spirit.
By it my faults are cured, my passions curbed, temptations overcome or weakened.' (ch. iv) Therefore he
must come, and come prepared—he must examine his
life and repent of every sin that would offend the eyes
of Christ, and must surrender himself wholly to his
will. Yet again he realizes his inability to do any of
this by his own strength—he is entirely dependent on
the grace of Christ. But the Beloved in mercy sends the
gift of grace, and the disciple is filled with wonder and

devotion. These two themes—grace and devotion—are woven into the whole texture of this book, for in the mind of the writer they are inextricably joined with the Sacrament, in which he finds his greatest joy.

In these four treatises the author has produced a handbook of practical ascetic discipline; he writes of the way of devotion, the inward life with its joys and griefs, its helps and hindrances. His approach is essentially practical not speculative, and firmly rooted in the realities of daily life. For this reason he makes no attempt to deal with theological or philosophical questions; it is clear that his basic approach is one of simple acceptance in faith of the traditional teaching of the Church, avoiding all debate on controversial topics. Such an attitude is not surprising in one so closely associated with the followers of Groote. Groote in his later years turned from secular learning and from the current forms of philosophical speculation on the grounds that they contributed nothing to man's spiritual well-being, and the *Imitation* more than once directly advocates such an attitude. We are there reminded of the dangers of worldly knowledge—the possibility of pride and the mind's distraction from its wholehearted search for God. The only important thing is to look to Christ and to seek to conform one's whole life in every detail to the pattern of his; the purpose of the four books is to provide a guide and encouragement based on personal experience to others who are seeking likewise to know the way of the cross.

The value of the *Imitation* lies in its relevance to the life of the ordinary Christian, not to any novelty of thought, even on the author's chosen theme. The work is a distillation of the atmosphere, beliefs and ideals of a whole religious movement—the mysticism and piety of the Netherlands and Rhineland in the fourteenth and fifteenth centuries—and in particular of the one manifestation of the movement, the Devotio Moderna, with which the author was himself concerned. The *Imitation* is considered to be the finest production of the Devotio Moderna, a work which crystallized the essential beliefs of the movement, and by its wide circulation helped to spread and perpetuate its influence.

Much that the *Imitation* contains is part of the general mystic tradition from early times; much stems from the sources that contributed immediately to the Devotio Moderna. While Groote and his followers turned from secular knowledge, they read widely in the Church Fathers and in devotional and mystic literature, and the marks of this are to be found on every page of the *Imitation,* where there are countless echoes of other writers. To a certain extent the work could be said to be made up of quotations—the very phrase 'the imitation of Christ' which now characterizes the whole book was by no means an invention of the author. The manner of quotation shows, however, the nature of the debt to other writers. This is no mere collection of excerpts. Few of the quotations are acknowledged and given verbatim. More often it is a case of reminiscence of wording or thought, of the combining together of two similar phrases. This suggests a familiarity with previous writers such that the words they use have become part of the author's own mental equipment. This is obviously the case of the Biblical quotations which abound in the *Imitation*; the words of Scripture are often completely fused with the text.

The following list, which is by no means complete, gives some of the authors whose writings have contributed in some measure to the formation of the *Imitation* : St Augustine, St Gregory, St Bernard, St Benedict, Hugh of St Victor, St Thomas Aquinas, Eckhart, Suso, Tauler, and the anonymous *Theologia Germanica*. The few quotations from classical literature that appear

in the *Imitation* are probably derived not so much from
first-hand study of the texts as from other medieval
writers or from the collections of pithy sayings that the
Brethren of the Common Life were accustomed to
make.[10]

Although much of the *Imitation* is unoriginal, the
personal note that pervades it gives it vitality and authority. The author does not thrust his own personality
forward, but one receives the impression that what he
writes has been tested in his own experience, and that
he has known in his own life the joys and sorrows which
he describes. In particular one is impressed by the
warmth of feeling that fills the whole work and reveals
the personality behind the words. One sees a man of
simple trust and faith, patient, gentle, kindly, desiring
that all shall set out on the way of perfection, a man
above all filled with a love and devotion to Christ that
spontaneously bursts out into prayer or praise. It is this
sense of reality together with its practical relevance to
everyday life that has given the work its well-merited
popularity.

Not a little of its immediate appeal must, however,
have depended on the style of the Latin in which it is
written, for the author has clearly given much thought
to the polishing and perfecting of the text. The *Imitation* is composed largely of short pithy sentences that
in general style recall the Book of Proverbs with their
conciseness and power of striking home and remaining

---

[10] In the translation of the Scriptural quotations the English version of the Bible by Monsignor Ronald Knox has been
used. Where the writer of the *Imitation* has quoted the actual
words of the Vulgate, the corresponding Knox version is given
in italics; where we find only a reminiscence of Biblical wording or a conflation of two texts, the translation has been com-
pounded from the Knox version of the appropriate verses and
italics have not been used. References have been given in the
footnotes to as many as possible of the Biblical quotations, both
direct and indirect, and also to some of the non-Biblical ones.

in the memory. Much of their effectiveness depends on
the employment of carefully balanced phrases in which
the number of words is kept approximately equal and
the antithesis pointed by the use of alliteration and
especially of rhyme. Another frequently used stylistic
device is the emphatic repetition of a group of words or
a similar construction in a number of succeeding sentences. It is clear that no word has been written hap-
hazardly or hastily, but given its place with careful
consideration of the total effect of the words in combination. The result is a rhythmical prose with many
of the beauties of poetry. Yet all this is achieved in
combination with a delightful simplicity and clarity,
which can best be illustrated by quotations from the
original :

Book I, I Haec sunt verba Christi quibus admonemur,
    quatenus vitam eius et mores imitemur :
    si velimus veraciter illuminari,
    et ab omni caecitate cordis liberari.[11]

Book I, III Certe adveniente die iudicii non quaeretur
    a nobis quid legimus sed quid fecimus ⸎
    nec quam bene diximus :
    sed quam religiose viximus.

[11] This manner of printing the text in short lines is that
adopted by Dr Karl Hirsche in his 1874 edition from the autograph manuscript of 1441, and is intended to demonstrate the
significance of the scheme of punctuation he discovered in that
manuscript. (The text is written continuously in the original
document.) According to his interpretation, there are four
punctuation marks indicating pauses of different lengths to be
observed in reading the text. Beginning with the shortest
these are (1) comma (2) colon (3) flexus ⸎ (v. examples 2, 3, 4)
(4) full stop. Dr Hirsche's text has been used as the basis of
this translation.

Book 3, v   Amor modum saepe nescit :
               sed super omnem modum fervescit.
               Amor onus non sentit :
               labores non reputat,
               plus affectat quam valet ?
               de impossibilitate non causatur :
               quia cuncta sibi posse et licere arbitratur.

Book 4, vii Ingemisce et dole quod adhuc ita carnalis
                   sis et mundanus ?
               tam immortificatus a passionibus :
               tam plenus concupiscentiarum motibus,
               tam incustoditus in sensibus exterioribus ?
               tam saepe multis vanis phantasiis impli-
                   catus :
               tam multum inclinatus ad exteriora,
               tam negligens ad interiora ?
               tam levis ad risum et dissolutionem :
               tam durus ad fletum et compunctionem
                                      etc.

    This style is in many ways natural to the Latin lan-
guage and it is difficult to find an equivalent in English
that does not sound highly artificial. Consequently no
attempt has been made in translation to reproduce much
of the word-play, though sentence rhythms have been
used that may represent in English something of the
effect of the Latin.

Glasgow, March 1963   B.I.K.

BOOK I

SOME THOUGHTS TO HELP WITH THE SPIRITUAL LIFE

I

On imitating Christ and rejecting all the folly and unreality of this world

He who follows me can never walk in darkness,[1] says the Lord.

By these words, Christ urges us to mould our lives and characters in the image of his, if we wish to be truly enlightened and freed from all blindness of heart. Let us therefore see that we endeavour beyond all else to meditate on the life of Jesus Christ.

Christ's teaching is better than all the teaching of the saints, and any man who has the Spirit will find *the hidden manna*[2] there. It so happens that many people hear the Gospel frequently and yet feel little desire, and this is because they do not have the Spirit of Christ. Anyone who wishes to understand and to savour the words of Christ to the full must try to make his whole life conform to the pattern of Christ's life.

What good can it do you to discuss the mystery of God the Trinity in learned terms if you lack humility and so displease that God? Learned arguments do not make a man holy and righteous, whereas a good life makes him dear to God. I would rather feel compunction in my heart than be able to define it. If you knew the whole Bible off by heart and all the expositions of scholars, what good would it do you without the love and grace of God?

[1] John 8.12   [2] Apoc. 2.17

A shadow's shadow—a world of shadows.[3] There is
no reality in anything except loving God and serving
him alone. Our highest wisdom is to seek the kingdom
of heaven, rejecting the things of this world. You are
only pursuing an empty phantom if you strive for riches
that cannot last, and pin your hopes on them; if you
canvass for honours and acquire distinction; if you
obey your natural appetites and desire things which
must bring punishment later; if you hope for a long
life and care little for a good life; if you think only of
this present life, and never give a thought to what comes
after it; if you set your heart on things which pass
away so quickly, and do not press on towards that place
where lasting joy remains.

Call often to mind that old saying—*eye looks on
unsatisfied, ear listens ill content.*[4] Make it your aim
to detach your heart from the love of things which can
be seen, and to transfer all your affections to things
which cannot be seen; for those who follow the impulses
of their senses stain their conscience and lose the grace
of God.

II

On having a humble opinion of oneself

Man has a natural desire for knowledge,[1] but what is
the good of knowledge without the fear of God? A
humble ignorant man who serves God is better than a
proud scholar who observes the movements of the
heavens and never gives a thought to his soul.[2] A man
who really knows his own nature sets no value on himself, and takes no pleasure in being praised by men.

[3] Eccles. 1.2   [4] Eccles. 1.8
[1] Aristotle, *Metaphysics* 1.1
[2] cf. Augustine, *Confessions* 5.4

Even if I know everything in the world, if I do not have love,[3] what good will it do me in the presence of God, who will judge me by what I have done?

Give up this passionate desire for knowledge, because it distracts you and leads you astray. Learned people like to be admired and acquire a name for wisdom, yet there are many things which it does little or no good to the soul to know, and a man is a fool to give his thoughts to things that contribute nothing to his salvation, instead of those that do. The soul is not satisfied by words in their thousands, whereas a good life sets the mind at rest, and a pure conscience gives assurance before God.

Unless your life shows a corresponding growth in holiness, increased knowledge and better understanding will only mean severer judgment. So you should not let skill or knowledge elate you, but should rather feel a certain apprehension at what you have been allowed to learn.

If you think you have a fair knowledge and understanding of a number of subjects, let me remind you that there are many more of which you know nothing. *Thou hast no reason for pride*[4]—but reason enough for acknowledging ignorance. What makes you want to put yourself in front of another man, when there are many people who are more learned than you and better versed in the Scriptures? If you want to learn something that will really help you, 'Aim at being unknown and thought of no account.'[5]

The highest and most profitable form of study is to understand one's inmost nature and despise it; real wisdom and perfection lie in having no high opinion of oneself, but in always thinking highly of others. Even if

[3] I Cor. 13.2   [4] Rom. 11.20
[5] This precept was often quoted by the Brethren of the Common Life. *v.* Thomas à Kempis, *Chronicle of Mount St Agnes,* ch. 3; *Alphabetum Monarchi* 1.

you see another man openly doing wrong, or committing some fault, you should not consider yourself a better man than he is, for you do not know how long you can avoid a fall. We are all of us weak, but you should consider yourself the weakest of all.

III

On being taught by Truth

How happy a man is when the Truth teaches him directly, not through symbols and words that are soon forgotten, but by contact with itself. Our own way of thinking and our own impressions give us only a false or limited view.

What is the point of a great argument about abstruse and difficult matters, when no one will be charged at the judgment with being ignorant of them? It is very foolish of us to neglect what is profitable and necessary, and deliberately to devote our attention to what is harmful and unnecessary. We have sightless eyes indeed.[1] Why do we trouble ourselves with theories about *genera* and *species*?[2]

If the eternal Word speaks to a man he is delivered from many conjectures. That one Word is the source of all things, and all things speak of that Word. That Word is the Beginning, and that Word speaks to us.[3] All understanding and all right judgment are derived from him. When a man sees all things as that one Word, refers all things to that one Word, views all

[1] Jer. 5.21
[2] Terms used in Aristotelian metaphysics to define the nature of reality and being. They were essential to the Aristotelian system, and would be familiar to anyone who had made even an elementary study of philosophy.
[3] John 8.25

things in that one Word, then he can be inwardly stable and rest at peace in God.

O God the Truth, unite me with yourself in ever-lasting love. I often grow tired of reading and hearing so much—in you lies all I really wish or desire. Let all teachers fall silent, let every creature hold its peace before you. Speak to me yourself, and speak alone.

As a man grows in inward unity and simplicity, he finds that more and more deep truths are made plain to him without any effort, because a heaven-sent light brings him understanding. The spirit that is pure, unified and stable does not lose its inward harmony, whatever it may do, for such a spirit does everything so as to honour God, and strives to be free from all self-seeking.

What causes you most hindrance and trouble is the fact that your own inclinations and desires are still very much alive. The good devout[4] man first puts right within him the impulses from which his outward actions proceed; and nothing that he does can put him at the mercy of corrupt desire, because he makes all his actions conform to the dictates of reason.

No one has a harder struggle than the man who is striving to overcome himself; and it should be our busi-ness to overcome ourselves, and every day to get the upper hand over our old nature, and to show some progress and improvement.

Everything that is perfect in this life has some imper-fection bound up with it, and there is nothing we inves-tigate that is without its darkness. Humble recognition of what your nature is will lead more surely to God than profound searching for knowledge. Learning or the simple knowledge of facts can be good and instituted by God, and then there is no fault to be found with it,

[4] v. Introduction, p. 13-14

but a good conscience and a holy life must always be preferred. Many people go wrong because they are more eager to acquire knowledge than to lead good lives, and so they bear little or no fruit. If only they showed as much determination in rooting out sins and ingrafting virtues as they do in debating, there would not be so many evils and scandals among the laity, nor so much lack of discipline in religious houses. When the day of judgment comes, we shall not be asked what we have read, but what we have done, not if we made fine speeches, but if we lived religious lives.

Tell me what has become of all those distinguished scholars and teachers who were so well known while they were still alive. Other men have their places now, and I doubt if they ever give them a thought. During their lifetime they were thought to be something, yet no one speaks of them now. How quickly the glory of this world fades away! If only their lives had matched their learning—then they would have read and studied to some good purpose. Many perish because they are filled with empty knowledge in this life and care little for the service of God. They choose to be great rather than humble, and so become *fantastic in their notions*.[5]

A really great man has great love. A really great man is humble in his own eyes, and considers all distinction and honour worthless. A really wise man treats all earthly things as refuse in order to have Christ to his credit.[6] A man who has really learnt something is one who does the will of God and abandons his own will.

[5] Rom. 1.21   [6] Phil. 3.8

IV

On thinking before acting

We do well to believe less than we are told,[1] and to
keep a wary eye on our own impulses; whatever it is,
we should think the matter over slowly and carefully,
referring it to God.

Unfortunately our weakness is such that we are much
more ready to believe and speak evil of others than
good. Yet perfect men do not lightly believe everyone
who chatters to them, since they know that human
nature is weak and inclined to evil, and very easily
betrayed into slips of the tongue.

It is wise neither to be impetuous, nor to hold obstin-
ately to your own opinions. This means firstly that you
should not believe any chance thing that is said to you,
nor should you immediately pour out into another's ears
something you have overheard or have been told.
Secondly, you should ask the advice of men who are
wise and conscientious, and be ready to be guided by
a better man, instead of following your own devices.

It is a good life that makes a man wise by God's
standards; it means that he learns from experience.[2]
Only if a man is humble and subject to God can he
behave with wisdom and calm in every circumstance.

[1] Ecclesiasticus 19.16   [2] Ecclesiasticus 34.9

V

On reading the Holy Scriptures

In the Holy Scriptures we must look for truth, not eloquence. All Scripture must be read in the spirit in which it is written, and in the Scriptures we should look for what will help us, and not for subtle points.

We should be just as ready to read devout simple books as deep and learned ones. You must not take offence at the writer's lack of learning and question his authority, but read the book from love of simple truth. Do not ask who it was that wrote it, but what it was he wrote. Men pass away, but *the Lord remains faithful to his word for ever.*[1] God uses all kinds of ways to speak to us, and he *makes no distinction between man and man.*[2]

When we read the Scriptures, we are often hindered by our curiosity, because we want to know and discuss where we ought simply to read on. If you want to drink in spiritual benefit, read in humility, simplicity and faith, and at no point desire to be known for your learning. Be glad to inquire from holy men, and listen to their answers in silence. Do not take offence at what the wise have to tell you, for they have good reason for what they say.[3]

[1] Ps. 116.2 [2] Acts 10.34; Gal. 2.6; and *passim.*
[3] Ecclesiasticus 32.12-13

VI

On an undisciplined frame of mind

Whenever a man feels an undisciplined desire for something, his spirit at once becomes restless. The proud and covetous are never at rest, but the poor and humble in spirit pass their lives in abundance of peace.

The man who is not yet perfectly dead to self is easily tempted; small and petty things defeat him. If a man is spiritually weak and to some extent still subject to his flesh and inclined to tangible things, it is difficult for him to free himself altogether from worldly desires; he is often miserable if he does try to give them up. Also he easily takes offence if anyone does not fall in with his wishes. If on the other hand he gets what he longs for, his guilty conscience weighs him down at once because he has given way to his natural impulses, which are no help at all towards the peace he sought.

So it is by resisting the desires that true peace of heart is found, not by yielding to them. That is why there is no peace in the heart of a man who is ruled by his natural desires and prisoner to externals; but there is peace in the man who is spiritually alive and ruled by spiritual standards.

VII

On avoiding empty confidence and pride

A man is a fool if he pins his hopes either on men or things. For love of Jesus Christ, you must be prepared to be a servant to other people, and to do without this world's possessions.

Do not make a stand on your own resources, but build your hopes on God. Do the best you can, and God will support your good intention. Do not rely on your own experience or anyone's worldly wisdom, but rely on the grace of God, who helps the lowly and humbles the presumptuous.

Do not glory in riches if you have them, nor in powerful friends; but glory in God who provides all, and above all, desires to impart himself.

Do not exult in a well-formed, beautiful body, for it only needs a little sickness to spoil and shatter it.

Do not let your abilities and mental powers make you pleased with yourself, or you may displease God to whom belong all the gifts given you by nature.

Do not think yourself better than others, or God may think you worse, for he knows what lies in man. Do not let your good works fill you with pride, because God does not judge like men. Men are often pleased by the things that displease him. If you have some good gift, believe that others have better gifts, and so you will keep humble. It does no harm to think yourself inferior to every other person, but it does a great deal of harm if you think yourself superior even to one other person.[1] The humble man knows continual peace, but in the heart of the proud there is often jealousy and discontent.

[1] v. St Bernard, *Sermons (in Cantica* 37.7, Migne P.L. 183, col. 974).

VIII

On avoiding excessive familiarity

It is not to every person that you are to lay bare your inmost thoughts;[1] discuss your business with a man who is wise and God-fearing.

Do not mix with young people and those outside the monastery.

Do not curry favour with the rich, and do not appear willingly in the company of the great. Make your companions the lowly and the unpretentious, the devout and law-abiding, and talk of the things that will build up faith.

You should not be on familiar terms with any woman, but commend all good women together to God.

You should want only God and his angels to know you well, and should shun the notice of men. Love you should feel for all people, but it is not good for you to be familiar with all. It sometimes happens that someone we do not know personally has a shining reputation, but if we meet him we find he is an eyesore; in the same way we think other people find pleasure in our company, but really they dislike us when they see our faulty lives.

[1] Ecclesiasticus 8.22

47

IX

On obedience and submission

It is a great thing to be in obedience, to live under a superior and give up one's independence. It is much safer to submit to authority than to exercise it.

Many are under authority from necessity rather than love, and such people suffer misery and soon begin to complain. They will never attain freedom of mind unless they submit wholeheartedly for the sake of God. You can run from one place to another, but you will find peace only in humble submission, under the direction of a superior. Many people have been deceived by fancying other places and by moving about.

Every one of us likes to do what he himself thinks best, and we tend to side with those who agree with us. Yet if God is among us, it is sometimes necessary to abandon our own convictions to keep the blessing of peace. No one is wise enough to know every detail and circumstance; so you must not rely exclusively on your own judgment, but be prepared to hear what others think.

If your own opinion is a valid one, and for God's sake you give it up in favour of another's, you will make great progress by it. I have often heard it said that it is safer to listen and receive advice than give it.

It can also happen that each man's opinion is a sound one, but it is a sign of obstinacy and pride to be unwilling to give way to others when reason and circumstance demand it.

X

On avoiding unnecessary talk

As far as possible avoid the company of men, for it is a great hindrance to talk of worldly affairs, even if you do it with an honest intention. It does not take long for empty pursuits to defile and capture us again. There are many occasions when I wish I had kept my silence unbroken, and had not mixed with men.

Why are we so ready to talk and chat with other people, when we rarely return to our silence without some injury to our conscience? We do it because we hope to receive some comfort from our conversation together, and because we want to unburden our hearts which are full of all the things we have thought. We are only too glad to fill our thoughts with the things we love or desire or find difficult, and to talk to others about them. The pity is that it is so often silly and useless to do so, for this outward comfort can destroy the inward comfort that is the gift of God.

We must watch and pray therefore, so that time is not wasted. If you have permission to speak and it is for your good to do so, talk of things which will strengthen faith. Bad habits and lack of concern for spiritual progress make us careless in guarding our lips; but if spiritual things are discussed together devoutly, especially where men of one mind and spirit enjoy fellowship together in God, then spiritual progress is furthered.

XI

On peace and eagerness for spiritual progress

We could have great peace, if we were prepared to abandon our curiosity about other people's words and actions, and things which are no business of ours. How can a man remain at peace for any length of time if he involves himself in the affairs of others and is always looking for a chance to interfere in the world around him and hardly ever withdraws into himself and quietens all his thoughts? It is the single-minded who are blessed, for they shall have peace in all its fullness.

How was it that some of the saints reached such heights of perfection and contemplation? They strove to die completely to every earthly longing, and so they were able to hold fast to God with all their inmost heart and concentrate without hindrance on the life within.

We are too much occupied with our own emotions, too much concerned with transitory things. It is rare for us to overcome even one fault completely, and we are not on fire to make daily progress. That is why we remain cold and uninspired. If we were utterly dead to self, and if our hearts were stripped of encumbrance, then we could get a glimpse of the things of God, and experience something of heavenly contemplation.

Our chief and greatest stumbling-block is that we are not free from emotions and desires, and we do not attempt to enter on the perfect way of the saints. When even a slight adversity befalls us, we are far too ready to be cast down and to turn to human comfort.

If only we would make an effort to stand firm in the battle, then we would assuredly see the help of the

Lord coming down on us from heaven. He is ready to help those who are struggling and hoping in his grace, for he provides opportunities for battle in order that we may be victorious.

If we think progress in our calling depends merely on outward observances, there will soon be an end to our devotion.[1] We must lay the axe to the root of the tree, so that we may be cleansed from our passions and possess a mind at peace. If we rooted out one failing every year we should soon be perfect men. But as it is, we often experience quite the opposite—we discover that we were better and purer men when we were first converted from the world than now, after many years of monastic life. Fervour and progress ought to be greater every day, but it is thought an achievement now if a man can retain even some of his first enthusiasm.

If we would only be firm with ourselves at first, everything afterwards would be easy and delightful. It is hard to give up something you are used to, and even harder to go against your own will; but how are you ever going to overcome hard things if you do not defeat little easy ones? You must resist the impulse and unlearn the bad habit in the early stages; otherwise it may turn into something much harder to deal with.

If only you realized what peace you could give yourself and what joy you could give to others by practising self-discipline, I think you would be more anxious to show some spiritual progress.

[1] v. Introduction, p. 13 n. 3

XII

On the benefits to be gained from meeting difficulty

It is a good thing that we have to face difficulties and opposition from time to time, because this brings us back to ourselves; it makes us realize that we are exiles and cannot pin our hopes on anything in this world.

It is a good thing that we are maligned now and again, and are misjudged and disliked even when we mean and do well. This sort of thing is often a great help in achieving humility, and it keeps us from groundless self-satisfaction; for we are more ready to listen for God's assuring voice within, when those around believe the worst of us and treat us with contempt. That is why a man should build his life on God, for then he will not need to look for human consolation.

When troubles and temptations and evil thoughts attack a man who is trying to do God's will, they make him realize how necessary God is to him, since he can do no good without him. The miseries he is enduring fill him with grief, and he groans and prays; he feels weary of life and longs for death to come, so that he may have done with this world and go to be with Christ.[1] At such times he really sees that perfect tranquillity and fullness of peace cannot exist in this world.

[1] Philipp. 1.23

XIII

On resisting temptation

As long as we are in this world we shall have to face trials and temptations. As it says in the Book of Job —What is man's life on earth but a time of temptation?[1] That is why we should treat our temptations as a serious matter and endeavour by vigilance and prayer to keep the devil from finding any loophole. Remember that the devil never sleeps, but goes about looking for his prey.[2] There is no one so perfect and holy that he never meets temptation; we cannot escape it altogether.

Yet temptations often bring great benefits, even if they are disagreeable and a great burden; for in temptation a man is humbled, purified and disciplined. All the saints passed through many trials and temptations, and that was how they made spiritual progress, while those who could not stand up to temptation fell away and lost their salvation.

However holy a religious order may be, however remote a place, temptations and difficulties will still be found there. Man is not entirely safe from temptation as long as he is alive, because the source of temptation lies within us—we are born in concupiscence. When one trial or temptation leaves us, another takes its place, and we will always have something to endure, because we have lost the blessing of human happiness.

Many people try to run away from temptation and all they do is fall more heavily. We cannot be victorious if we only run away, but patience and true humility will give us strength to defeat every enemy.

[1] Job 7.1   [2] I Peter 5.8

A man will not make much progress if he rejects the actual temptation but fails to root out its cause. The temptation will soon come back and he will suffer worse.

It is by slow degrees, by patience and long-suffering with the help of God that you will win the victory, not by harshness and impatience. When you are tempted, seek guidance often from others; and do not yourself deal harshly with someone else who is tempted, but comfort him, as you would wish to be comforted yourself.

The starting-point of all evil temptings lies in inconstancy of mind and small confidence in God. The slack man who abandons his fixed resolve is battered by all kinds of temptation like a ship with no steersman, driven to and fro by the waves.

Iron is proved in the fire, and the upright man in temptation. We often do not know what we are capable of till temptation reveals what kind of persons we are.

All the same, when temptation first appears, we must be especially alert, because it is easier to defeat the enemy if we do not allow him to set foot inside the door of the mind but meet him on the step as he knocks. As an ancient writer once said : Resist the beginnings— cure is provided too late.[8] For first of all, a thought simply crosses the mind, then it grows stronger and takes shape; then comes pleasure, an evil impulse, and consent. So our malignant enemy gradually obtains complete entry if we do not resist him at the start. If a man is slow in stirring himself up to resist, he will grow weaker every day, while the enemy forces grow stronger.

Some people endure harder temptations when they are first converted, some at the end. Some find things difficult throughout their whole lives, while a few are tried very mildly. God in his wisdom and justice has so

[8] Ovid, *Remedium Amoris* 1.91

decreed it, and he weighs the situation and the merits of men, and fore-ordains everything for the salvation of his elect.

For this reason we should not despair when tempted, but beseech God all the more fervently to aid us in his mercy in every kind of distress; for as Paul says, *With the temptation itself, he will ordain the issue of it, and enable you to hold your own.*[4]

So let us humble our souls under the hand of God in every temptation and trouble, for he will save and exalt those who are humble in spirit. Trials and temptations test what progress a man has made; it is there that merit is found, and virtue better revealed. It is no great thing for a man to feel fervour and devotion to God when he is not troubled; but if he patiently maintains his spiritual state in a time of adversity, then there is hope of great progress.

Some people are kept from great temptations, and yet are defeated in the little affairs of every day. This humbles them and teaches them never to rely on themselves where important things are concerned, since they are found so weak in unimportant ones.

XIV

On avoiding hasty judgments

Turn your eyes on yourself, and beware of judging the actions of others. In judging others a man expends effort to no purpose, he is often mistaken and easily sins; but in judging himself and in scrutinizing his own actions he is always exerting himself profitably.

Our feelings about anything often affect the way we judge it, because it is easy to lose the faculty of honest judgment through self-interest. If God were always the

[4] I Cor. 10.13

pure purpose of all our desires it would not be so easy for our own feelings to resist and throw us into confusion; but as it is, there is something that carries us along with it, whether it lurks in our own hearts or affects us from outside.

Many people are not aware that they are secretly pursuing their own interest in what they are doing. They give the impression of deep unshakeable peace, as long as life brings what they want and behaves the way they think it should; but the moment things cease to go the way they want, we find them upset and unhappy.

It is differences of feeling and opinion that so often cause dissension among friends and fellow-citizens, among the religious and devout. This is because it is difficult to abandon a belief of long standing, and because no one is easily persuaded to accept a new point of view.

If you rely on your own reason and efforts rather than on the submissive virtue of Jesus Christ, it will be a long slow process before you are spiritually enlightened. God wants us to be perfectly submitted to him, and to transcend all human reason through the burning flame of love.

XV

On good works springing from love

An evil deed must not be committed for anything in the world, not even from affection for anyone; but for the good of someone in need a good work may sometimes be left undone, or exchanged for a better one. In this way, the good work is not destroyed, but changed into something better.

A good deed done without love goes for nothing, but

if anything is done from love, however small and incon-
siderable it may be, every bit of it is counted. God
considers what lies behind the deed, and not what is
actually done.

A man does much if he has much love. A man does
much if he does what he has to do well. A man does
well if he does the will of the community and not his
own will.

Often what seems to be love is really an unspiritual
emotion, because there is usually some trace of natural
inclination, our own wishes, the hope of repayment,
and the desire to further our own ends.

The man who has true and perfect love does not seek
his own advantage in anything, but desires only that
God may be glorified in all things. He feels no envy
towards anyone, because he has no desire for any
pleasure that is not shared; nor does he want any joy
that springs from self, because he desires to find his
happiness above all good gifts in God. Goodness he
does not attribute to any man, but ascribes it wholly to
God, the Source from whom all things proceed, the
End in whom all the saints rest and find their delight.

Anyone who had a spark of the true love would
surely know that everything on earth was deceptive and
unreal.

XVI

On bearing with the failings of others

The things a man is unable to put right either in himself or in others he must endure until it is God's will to
change them. Reflect that a situation like this is more
likely to test you and teach you patience—and without
patience we have no merits worth considering. Still,
you should pray about the things that are a problem to

you, asking God in his mercy to help you bear them with kindliness. If anyone does not comply when you have urged him once or twice, do not argue with him, but commit the whole situation to God, who knows how to turn evil into good, so that his will may be done in all his servants, and honour brought to his name.

Try to be patient in bearing with the failings and weaknesses of other people, whatever they may be. You too have many faults, which others have to endure. If you cannot make yourself the kind of person you wish, how can you expect to have someone else to your liking? We want perfection in other people, and yet we do not put right our own failings. We want to see others firmly corrected, but we refuse correction ourselves. We take offence when permission is given to others, but we do not want our own requests refused. We want rules to check the activities of others, but we are indignant at restrictions on ourselves. It is clear how rarely we apply to our neighbours the same standards as ourselves.

If everyone were perfect, we should have nothing to bear from other people for the sake of God. As it is, he has made things the way they are so that we may learn to bear the burden of one another's failings.[1] There is no one free from weakness, no one without a load to carry, no one who is self-sufficient, no one who can dispense with others' help; and so it is our duty to support each other, to comfort each other, to help, guide and advise each other.

A man's true quality is revealed when things are difficult. Events do not make a man weak—they only show what stuff he is made of.

[1] Gal. 6.2

XVII

The monastic life

You must learn to crush your natural feelings on all sorts of occasions if you wish to live with others in unbroken peace and concord. It is no small thing to live in a monastery or religious community, and so spend your life there that you are beyond reproach,[1] and *keep faith to the point of death*.[2] A man is blessed if he can live well in such a place and continue well to the end.

If you wish to live as you ought and progress steadily, you must conduct yourself as an exile wandering on the earth.[3] You must become a fool for Christ's sake,[4] if you wish to live the religious life. The habit and the tonsure contribute little—it is the change of character and the killing of the old impulses that make the true religious.

A man who is looking for anything but God and the salvation of his soul will find nothing but sorrow and distress; neither can anyone long remain in peace, unless he is striving to be the least, subject to everyone else. You came to serve and not to rule. Understand that you were called to suffer and to work, not to waste time and gossip. Here men are put to the test like *gold tried in the crucible*.[5] Here no one can last unless he is prepared wholeheartedly to humble himself for God.

---

[1] Philipp. 3.6 [2] Apoc. 2.10 [3] Ps. 38.13; I Peter 2.11
[4] I Cor. 4.10 [5] Wisdom 3.6

XVIII

The example of the holy fathers

If you consider the vigorous example we have in the holy fathers who shone with true perfection and religion, you will see the insignificance and the nothingness of what we do. How far our way of life falls short of theirs! Those holy men and friends of Christ went hungry and thirsty, cold and naked; they met with toil and weariness, and denied themselves food and sleep; they gave themselves to prayer and holy meditation, and faced persecution and insult,[1] and so they served the Lord. How many bitter trials were endured by the apostles, martyrs, confessors and virgins, and all who desired to follow where Christ had led! They were enemies to their own lives in this world, in order to preserve their lives and live eternally.[2]

What a life of strict self-denial the fathers lived in the desert! What long hard temptations they endured, how often the Enemy harassed them! What frequent, burning prayers they offered to God, what rigorous abstinence they practised! How full of zeal and fervour they were for spiritual progress, how hard they fought to subdue their faults, how purely and unswervingly they directed their wills to God! By day they worked, and by night they spent long hours in prayer, though even while they were working they never ceased from praying mentally. Every moment they spent usefully; the time they could give to God seemed short to them, and in the great sweetness of contemplation they forgot the body's need of food. They renounced all possessions, rank, honours, friends and family, and wanted to have nothing to do with the world; they hardly took

[1] II Cor. 11.27; 12.10   [2] John 12.25

enough to keep themselves alive, and were sorry to attend to the body, even when it was unavoidable.

So they had little in the way of earthly possessions, but they had grace and virtue in plenty; they lived in material poverty, but in their hearts were enriched by the grace and comfort of God. They were strangers to the world, but to God they were close, familiar friends. In their own eyes they were nothing, and the world despised them, but in the eyes of God they were precious and beloved. They practised true humility, and lived in straightforward obedience. Their daily lives were filled with patience and love, and so every day they made some spiritual progress, and God was well pleased with them. They were given to be an example to all who follow the religious life; and we ought to find more of an incentive to progress in them, than an encouragement to slackness in the vast numbers of people who remain halfhearted.

What fervour there was in all religious when they first established their holy way of life! what devotion in prayer, what enthusiasm for virtue, what discipline, what reverence and obedience under the rule of the superior flourished among them all! There are traces still left to tell us that they were truly perfect and holy men, who fought with energy and trampled the world under foot.

But now a man is considered great if he manages not to do wrong, or if he can show some patience in enduring what he has undertaken. How lukewarm and indifferent our present state is—we fall away so quickly from our first enthusiasm, and by this time we are tired of living from our very weariness and lack of inspiration.

You have often enough seen the example of devout people. I hope you are still sufficiently awake to make some progress in virtue!

XIX

The exercises of a good religious

The life of a good religious should abound in all the virtues, so that he really is the kind of man he gives the impression of being. In fact, there ought to be much more in him than those around can see, because God is the one who really examines us, and we should feel awe towards him, wherever we may be, and should walk in purity before him like his angels.

Every day we should make a fresh resolve, and stir ourselves up to ardour as if we had just come to the monastery for the first time today. We should say : O Lord God, help me in my good resolve and in your holy service. Grant that I may this day make a real beginning, for what I have so far done is nothing.

Our progress depends upon our resolution, and a man who wishes to make good progress needs perseverance. If a man fails even when he sets his purpose firmly before him, what will happen to the man who does not often make a resolution and is not really determined about it? We fall short of our purpose in all kinds of ways, and even a slight omission in our exercises can hardly pass without some loss. The resolve of the upright depends on the grace of God, not on their own wisdom; in him they trust, whatever they undertake; for man proposes, God disposes, and *it is not for man to choose his lot*.[1]

If you sometimes omit your usual exercise for some spiritual reason, or for the good of a brother, it will be easy to resume it again afterwards; but it is very bad to abandon it out of carelessness or because you are

[1] Prov. 16.9; Jerem. 10.23

tired of it, and you will find you suffer for it. Even if we try as hard as we can, we will still often fail without much reason. We must always set some definite resolve before us, especially to combat the things that hinder us most.

Both our inward and our outward lives contribute to our progress, and so we must examine both and set both to rights. If you are not able to keep your thoughts collected all the time, concentrate them occasionally, and at least once a day, in the morning for example, or in the evening. In the morning resolve on your conduct for the day, in the evening review it. What kind of person did you show yourself today in word and thought and deed? In all of these you may have offended both God and your neighbour often.

Make a bold stand against the craftiness of the devil. Bridle your desire for food, and you will find it easier to bridle all the body's cravings. Never be completely idle, but be reading or writing, or praying or meditating, or working at something that will benefit the community. Yet physical exercise must be taken with discretion, and not equally by all.

Practices that are not shared by the whole community should not be paraded in public—your private devotions are best exercised in secret. All the same, you must beware of becoming careless about communal devotions because you feel more inclined to private ones. When you have fully and faithfully carried out what you are obliged and instructed to do, then, if there is any time left, you can give your attention to yourself as your devotion requires.

Not everyone can make use of the same exercise—some people are better served by one and some by another. Besides, different exercises suit better at different times. Some are more to our taste on feast days, others on ordinary days. We need some in time of

temptation, others in time of peace and quiet. There
are some things we are glad to think of when we are
sad, and others when we are glad in the Lord.

When the principal festivals come round, we should
make a fresh start with our good exercises, and implore
the intercession of the saints more earnestly than ever.
At every festival, we should make a resolution as if we
were now going to leave this world and come to the
eternal festival. At these times of devotion we should
prepare ourselves carefully, and live more devoutly, and
keep all our observances more strictly, as if we were
shortly going to receive the reward of our labours from
God. If it is delayed, we must suppose that we are not
sufficiently prepared, and are still unworthy of the
great *glory which is to be revealed in us*[2] at the appointed time, and we must try to make ourselves ready
to leave.

Blessed is that servant, says the evangelist Luke, *who
is found doing this when his lord comes. I promise you,
he will give him charge of all his goods.*[3]

XX

On loving solitude and silence

Make time to attend to your inner life, and frequently
think over the benefits God has given you. Abandon
those subjects you find so fascinating, and instead of
reading books which interest your mind, read those
which nourish compunction.[1] If you give up unnecessary conversation, idle walking about, and listening to
news and talk, you will find plenty of time which you
can well devote to good meditation.

The greatest of the saints avoided the company of

[2] Rom. 8.18   [3] Luke 12.43-4; cf. also Matt. 24.46-7
[1] *v.* Introduction, p. 28 n. 9

men as often as they could, and chose to serve God in secret. As somebody once said : If ever I go among men, I come back less of a man.[2] We often experience the truth of this if we chat together too long. It is easier to keep quiet altogether than not to say a word too much. It is easier to stay completely hidden, than to watch yourself if you go out. The man who intends to reach the inner castle of the spirit must, with Jesus, withdraw from the crowd.[3]

No one can safely go among men but the man who loves solitude. No one can safely speak, but the man who loves silence. No one can safely be in command, but the man who has learned complete obedience. No one can safely rejoice unless he has within him the witness of a good conscience.

Yet the security of the saints was always full of the fear of God, nor were they any the less careful and humble because they shone with virtue and grace. The security of the wicked comes from pride and presumption, and in the end it betrays them.

You must never expect security in this life, even if you are known as a good monk or a devout hermit. The people with the best reputations have often been in greatest danger, because they have become too self-confident. So for many people it is better if they are not free from temptation but are attacked often, as this prevents them from feeling too secure or becoming arrogant, or from turning aside easily to enjoy external comforts.

If only we never looked for transitory delights or concerned ourselves with the world—then we would keep our conscience clear ! If only we would prune away all our useless concerns, and think only of God and our salvation, and rest all our hopes on him—then we would know such depths of peace and quietness !

[2] v. Seneca, *Epistle* 7   [3] John 5.13

No one is fit for heavenly comfort unless he has made an effort to feel the holy emotion of compunction. If you desire to feel this compunction in your heart, go into your room and shut out the turmoil of the world. As the Bible says: *Take thought in the silence of your hearts.*[4] You will find in your cell what you will often lose outside. If you spend much time in your cell, it will become increasingly delightful to you, but if you absent yourself you will find you come to hate it. If when you are first converted you keep to it as much as you can, it will become your beloved friend and a place of joy and comfort. It is in the peace and quietness of the cell that the devout soul makes progress and learns the hidden truths of Scripture; it is there that it finds the floods of tears which will wash it clean every night; and as it withdraws from all the tumult of the world, it comes to know its Creator—for God and his holy angels will draw close to the man who withdraws from acquaintances and friends.

It is better to be hidden and to take thought for one's soul than to neglect oneself and work miracles. A religious deserves praise when he rarely goes outside, avoids being seen, and has no wish to see others.

Why do you want to see things that you may not possess? *The world and its gratifications pass away.*[5] It is the longings of the senses that induce us to go outside, but when the hour has passed, we come back with nothing but a burden on our conscience and turmoil in our hearts. A glad departure often leads to a sad return, and happiness in the evening makes the morning sad. Every unspiritual joy looks attractive as it first creeps in, but in the end it poisons and destroys. What can you see anywhere that you cannot see here? Here you have the sky, the earth, and all the elements as well, since they make everything. What can you see anywhere that the sun will shine on for long? You may think that if you saw it you would be content, but that will never be so; if everything that exists appeared before your eyes, it would be nothing but a spectacle that gave no satisfaction.

Lift your eyes to God in high heaven, and pray for the things you have done and left undone. Leave empty things to empty-minded people, and direct your thoughts to God's commands for you. Shut the door upon yourself, and invite in Jesus your beloved. Stay with him in your cell, for you will not find peace like that elsewhere. If you had never left your cell and never heard any news from outside, you would have remained at peace. If you take pleasure in hearing new things, you are bound to have your quiet of heart disturbed.

XXI

On compunction of heart

If you wish to make any progress, keep yourself in awe of God, and avoid excessive freedom of manner; see that all your senses are disciplined and held in check, and do not indulge in mistimed hilarity. Give yourself to compunction of heart, and then you will find devotion. Compunction will open the way to many blessings that you lose if you let yourself grow careless.

It would be a strange thing if any man could find this life a source of perfect happiness, if he seriously considered his exiled state and the many dangers that threaten his soul. But we are careless about our shortcomings and take everything so lightly, and so we do not feel our soul's distress. We often indulge in empty laughter when we have good reason to weep. Yet this is not real freedom or true happiness—that can only be found in awe of God and a good conscience.

The happy man is one who can shake off the burden of his disordered thoughts and concentrate every faculty in one holy emotion of compunction. The happy man is one who can discard everything that stains or burdens his conscience.

Be a man and make an effort—only a good habit can defeat a bad one.

If you are able to leave other people alone, they will leave you alone to do what you have to do. Do not make other people's affairs a part of your concern, and do not get yourself involved in important people's business. Always have an eye in the first place to yourself, and see that you give yourself advice before you give it to your friends.

If you are not popular with others, you should not let it make you unhappy; but you should be worried when you see that you are not living with the discipline and care proper to a servant of God and a devout religious. It is often better for a man, and safer, if he does not have many comforts in this life, especially the sort that please his natural instincts. All the same, if we do not have divine comfort, or if we experience it only rarely, we are to blame, because we do not endeavour to feel compunction in our hearts, nor do we reject all empty and external comforts. You must recognize that you are unworthy of the divine comfort, and that trials are what you deserve.

When a man achieves the state of true compunction, the whole world becomes a bitter burden to him.

The good man can find plenty to cause him sorrow and tears. He has only to consider himself or think of his neighbour, to realize that no one lives on this earth without distress; and the more closely he looks at himself, the more his grief increases. Our sins and failings give us good cause for sorrow and inner compunction, because we are so bound down by them that we are hardly ever able to raise our eyes to heavenly things.

If you gave more thought to your death and less to the years you still have left, you would certainly show more enthusiasm in putting right your faults. If you really thought seriously about the pains that await you in hell or purgatory, I am sure you would endure toil and suffering gladly, and would submit to any hardship without a moment's hesitation. It is because such thoughts do not penetrate to our hearts, and because we still love what is pleasant, that we remain so cold and apathetic.

Often it is because of our spiritual poverty that our wretched body complains so readily. So humbly pray the Lord that he will give you the spirit of compunction, and say with the prophet: Allot us, O Lord, *for food, for drink, only the full measure of our tears.*[1]

XXII

The miseries of our human state

You are a pitiable creature wherever you are and wherever you turn, unless you turn to God.

Why are you so disconcerted when things do not go the way you want them to? Does anyone have everything his own way? No, not you nor I, nor any man on earth. There is no one in this world who does not have some trouble and distress, not even a king or a Pope. Yet there is someone who is happier than others, and that is the man who is able to suffer for God.

You find many weak and foolish people who say, 'Look what a fine life that man has—he is rich and

[1] Ps. 79.6

great and powerful and distinguished.' Yet if you turn your eyes to heavenly blessings you will see that all these temporal things are not blessings at all. In fact, they are burdens, because they cannot be relied on, and because they always involve anxiety and fear. Man's happiness does not depend on an abundance of temporal possessions—a modest amount is sufficient for him.

It is a wretched thing to have to live on earth; life here becomes steadily more distasteful to anyone who is longing to be more spiritual, for such a person is always seeing more clearly and feeling more deeply the shortcomings of our mortal state; for eating and drinking, waking and sleeping, resting and working, and submitting to all that our body demands, proves a great hardship and misery to the devout man, who longs to have done with it all and be freed from all sin. The needs of the body in this world are certainly a great burden to the inner self. That is why the prophet prays devoutly that he might be freed from them, saying: *Deliver me from my distress, O Lord.*[1]

No good can befall those people who do not realize that their state is wretched; and this is even more true of those who actually love this wretched mortal life— some people are so attached to life, even if they can hardly get enough by working or begging to provide the bare necessities, that if they could live here for ever, they would never give a thought to the kingdom of God. What senseless and unbelieving men they are—they grovel in earthly concerns until they cannot appreciate anything that is not material. Yet in the end, these wretched people will find out to their cost how worthless and unreal were the things they loved.

On the other hand, the saints of God and all the devout friends of Christ paid no attention to the things that gratified their natural appetites, or to the fine

[1] Ps. 24.17

things of this world, but they set their eyes on the blessings of eternity, and hoped and longed for nothing else. Their desire was directed upwards towards the invisible things that endure, for fear that the love of visible things should drag them down to the depths.

My brother, do not throw away that confidence you have[2] of attaining spiritual things—there is still time and opportunity. But why put off making your resolve? Stand up and begin this moment; say to yourself : Now is the time for action, now is the time for battle, now is the right time to mend my ways.

When you are distressed and troubled, that is the time for winning merit. Your way must lead through fire and water before you are granted relief.[3] Unless you are cruel to your natural instincts, you will never get the better of your faults.

As long as we wear this feeble body, we cannot be free from sin, or live without weariness and suffering. We would like to escape from all our miseries and know peace, but when sin destroyed our innocence we lost true happiness as well. So we must hold on in patience, and wait for God's mercy, until the storms pass by[4] and our mortal nature is swallowed up in life.[5]

Human nature is so weak—it is always ready to sin. Today you confess your sins, and tomorrow you commit again the very sins you have just confessed. You resolve to be on your guard, and in an hour you are behaving as if you had never resolved. We may well feel ashamed and never think much of ourselves, when we are so weak and insecure. Besides, we can soon destroy through carelessness the very thing we have only just managed to achieve with much labour, and that with the help of grace.

What will happen to us later on, when we lose our enthusiasm so early in the day? No good will come to

[2] Hebr. 10.35   [3] Ps. 65.12   [4] Ps. 56.2   [5] II Cor. 5.4

us if we want to turn aside and rest as if peace and
security were here already, when so far there is not a
trace of true holiness in our lives. We might well be
treated like good novices and be put under instruction
again to learn right conduct, if there were any hope
that such a course would lead to our improvement and
greater spiritual progress.

XXIII

On considering one's death

Very soon all will be over for you in this life, so ask
yourself how you will fare in the next. A man is here
today and gone tomorrow, and once he is out of our
sight it is not long before he is out of our minds as well.

The human heart is so hard and unresponsive—it
only troubles about the present, with never a glance for
the future. In all your doing and thinking you should
act on the assumption that you are going to die today.
If you had a good conscience, death would hold no
great fears for you. You would do better to shrink from
sin than to run in fear from death. If you are not prepared for death today, are you likely to be prepared
tomorrow? Tomorrow is uncertain—how can you be
sure you will have a tomorrow?

What is the use of a long life when we show so little
improvement? Long life unfortunately does not always
improve us, but often piles up sins instead. If only we
had spent one single day well while on this earth!
Many people reckon up the years since their conversion,
but often there is not much of a harvest to show for it,
in the way of spiritual improvement. Death may well
be a dreadful thing—but possibly it is more hazardous
to remain alive.

A man is blessed if he is able to keep the hour of his

death continually before his eyes, and every day to hold himself in readiness for death. If you have ever seen a man die, recall that you too must travel the same road. In the morning think that you will not reach the evening; when evening comes, do not venture to assume the morning will be yours. Always be ready; live in such a way that death can never find you unprepared. Many die suddenly, and without warning, for *the Son of Man will come at an hour when you are not expecting him.*[1] When that last hour comes, you will begin to think very differently of all your past life, and will bitterly regret being so careless and remiss.

A man is not only happy but wise also, if he is trying during his lifetime to be the sort of man he wants to be found at his death. We can be sure of dying happily if our lives show an utter disregard of the world, a fervent desire for progress in virtue, a love of discipline, the practice of penitence, readiness to obey, denial of self, and acceptance of any adversity for the love of Christ.

While you are well, you can do many good works, but when you lose your health, I do not know that you will be able to do anything. Few people are improved by sickness, and it is not those who are always travelling about who grow in sanctity.

Do not rely on friends and acquaintances, nor leave your salvation to the future—men will forget you sooner than you think. It is better to take thought for the future while you still have time, and to lay up some treasure in advance, rather than leave it to what others can do. If you do not look after your own interests now, who will care for them when you are dead?

The present time is very precious—*here is the time of pardon; the day of salvation has come already.*[2] What a pity you do not make better use of the opportunity you now have of winning eternal life. The time will

[1] Luke 12.40   [2] II Cor. 6.2

come when you will long for one day, even for one
hour, to amend your life, and I fear you will not get it.
My dear friend, what fear you can save yourself, what
danger you can escape, if you only keep yourself God-
fearing and mindful of your death.

Try to live in such a way now that when the hour of
death comes you may feel joy, not fear. Learn to die to
the world now, so that you may begin to live with
Christ then. Learn not to value anything in this life
now, so that you can go to Christ without anything to
hinder you then. Subdue your body by penance now, so
that you may have unshakeable confidence then.

You fool, why do you imagine you will live a long
life, when you cannot be sure of a single day? Many
have made this mistake and have been snatched away
from life when they least expected it. So often you hear
people saying that so and so has been killed in battle,
and so and so drowned; another man has fallen from a
height and broken his neck; one choked over a meal,
another met his end in some sport. Others have died by
fire, by violence, by sickness, by robbery—death is the
end of all, and the life of man passes by and vanishes
like a shadow. Who will remember you after your
death, and who will pray for you then?

It is now, my dear friend, now, that you must do
anything that lies in your power to do; you have no
idea when you will die, nor what awaits you after
death. While you still have time, lay up riches that do
not pass away. Think of nothing but your salvation,
care for nothing but the things of God. Win friends
now for yourself by honouring the saints of God and
following their example, so that when you leave this
life behind they will welcome you into eternal habita-
tions.[8]

Remember all the time that you are a stranger and a
    [8] Luke 16.9

wanderer on the earth, with no concern in the affairs of
the world. Keep your near free and lifted up to God,
because you *have an everlasting city, but not here.*[4] It
is to that place that you must every day direct your
prayers, your sighs, your tears, so that after death your
soul may pass in gladness to the Lord. Amen.

XXIV

On judgment and the punishment of sinners

At all times, keep the end of your life in mind. How
will you stand before that stern Judge? Nothing is
concealed from him; he receives no bribes, and listens
to no excuses, but will give the judgment that is just.

You wretched, foolish sinner, you are sometimes
afraid to face a man who is angry with you, so what
reply will you make to God who knows all the wrong
you have done? Why do you not make some provision
for yourself in the day of judgment? No one can be
excused or defended by someone else then, but each one
of us will find himself enough to bear. It is your
labour now that is profitable, your tears now that are
acceptable, your laments now that are heard, your
sorrow now that atones and cleanses your soul.

The patient man is already experiencing a deep and
healthful purging. When he receives an injury, he is
more distressed for the other's unkind thought than for
the hurt he has received; he gladly prays for those who
put obstacles in his path, forgives others their faults
from his heart, and is not slow in seeking their forgive-
ness. He is more ready to feel pity for others than
anger, but his own feelings he often treats roughly, and

[4] Hebr. 13.14

he tries to keep his natural impulses obedient to his spirit.

It is better to prune out sins and cut out faults now, than to preserve them for purifying later. We certainly let ourselves be blinded by the undisciplined affection we harbour for our old corrupt nature. What will that fire consume, unless it is your sins? The more you spare yourself now and follow your natural appetites, the heavier the penalty you will pay later, the more fuel you keep for the fire.

Each man's particular punishment will depend on his sins. Those who give way to despair and apathy will be stirred up with burning goads, and the gluttonous tormented with hunger and thirst. Lovers of luxury and pleasure will be drenched in burning pitch and stinking sulphur, and the envious will howl in pain like mad dogs. No sin will be without its appropriate torment. The proud will be utterly humiliated, and the avaricious feel the pinch of direst poverty. One hour in torment there will be harder to bear than a hundred years under the heaviest penance here. There is no respite there, no solace for the damned; but here there is sometimes relief from toil, and we know the pleasure and comfort of friendship.

You must feel concern and sorrow now for your sins, so that in the day of judgment you may be safe with the blessed. *How boldly then will the just man appear to meet his old persecutors,*[1] those who ground him down! Then the man who now submits himself humbly to the judgments of men will stand up to judge others. Then the poor and humble will have great confidence, and the proud will feel fear on every side. Then it will be seen that the man who learned to be a fool and to be despised for Christ's sake was the one who was wise in this world. Then every trial patiently endured will bring its reward, and *malice stand dumb with confu-*

[1] Wisdom 5.1

sion.[2] Then every devout man will rejoice and every irreligious one will mourn. Then the flesh that has suffered will triumph more than if it had been always reared in luxury. Then a coarse habit will be resplendent and the glory of fine clothing will be dimmed. Then a poor cottage will find more praise than a golden palace. Then patience and constancy will help us more than all the power of this world. Then straightforward obedience will be exalted above all worldly wisdom. Then a good pure conscience will bring more happiness than deep learning. Then contempt of wealth will carry more weight than all the treasures of the races of earth. Then you will find more comfort from your devout prayers than from elegant eating. Then you will feel more joy for silence preserved than for long talking. Then holy works will be of more value than many fine words. Then a disciplined life and hard penance will give more satisfaction than all the delights of earth.

You must learn to suffer now to a small extent, so that you can then escape far worse suffering. Let your experiences now reveal your strength for the future— if you are only able to bear such a little in this life, how will you be able to bear eternal torment? If such slight suffering now makes you so impatient, what will Gehenna do then? You may be sure of this—you cannot have two joys. You cannot have pleasure here in this world, and afterwards reign with Christ as well. If you had spent your whole life right up to this day amidst honour and pleasures, what good would it all do you if you were to die at this very instant?

There is no reality in anything except loving God and serving him alone; and so the man who loves God with his whole heart does not fear death or punishment, judgment or hell, because perfect love enables us to come to God without fear; but it is no wonder if the man who still finds pleasure in sinning is afraid of

[2] Ps. 106.42

death and judgment. All the same, it is a good thing if the fear of hell restrains you, if love cannot yet call you back from wrong. Indeed, anyone who rejects the fear of God will not be able to continue in what is good for long, but will soon fall into the snares of the Devil.

XXV

On being determined to amend our whole life

You must be watchful and diligent in the service of God, and frequently ask yourself why you came here, and why you left the world. Was it not in order to live for God and to become a spiritual man? You must therefore be eager to make spiritual progress, because it will not be long before you receive the reward of your labours, and then there will be no more fear or pain within your boundaries.

Unlaborious days, what a harvest they will win you of repose![1] More than that, they will bring you never-ending joy. If you remain faithful and earnest in all you do, God will certainly be faithful and generous in giving you your reward. You must never cease to hope that you will win your prize, though you must never assume that you will win it; otherwise you may become arrogant or careless.

There was once a man who worried about this, and he tossed between hope and fear. Worn out with misery, he threw himself down one day to pray before an altar in the church, and as he turned the problem over in his mind, he said, 'If only I could know that I would go on persevering.' Immediately he was aware of God's reply within him—'What would you do if you did know? Do in any case what you would do then, and you will be free from care.' At once he was com-

[1] Ecclesiasticus 51.35

forted and strengthened, and entrusted himself to the will of God, and his anxious tossings ceased. He no longer had any curiosity about what the future held for him, but was eager to discover what was *God's will, the desirable thing, the perfect thing,*[2] so that he might begin and complete every work that was good.

Be content to trust in the Lord and do good, says the prophet, *live on thy land . . . so he will give thee what thy heart desires.*[3]

There is one thing which keeps many people back from progress and eagerness to amend—they shrink from difficulty and they know the struggle is hard. It is the people who make an effort to overcome things they find difficult and repugnant who make more progress than the rest in virtue; a man makes progress and merits grace above all in those points where he has to overcome his own nature and die to the claims of self. Some people do not have as much to overcome as others, and their old nature is not so hard to kill; but a man who is making a determined effort will be better fitted to make progress, even if he is subject to many violent feelings, than another man who is under better control but is less enthusiastic about attaining virtue.

There are two things that help us especially to improve our lives : we must forcibly withdraw from the things to which our sinful nature inclines, and eagerly seek the virtue in which we are deficient.

You must also take care to be on your guard and to overcome those things especially which displease you most often in others. You may find opportunities for progress everywhere—if you see or hear of good examples, you should be inspired to follow them; if you observe anything that can be blamed, take care that you do not do the same. If you have ever done it, you must quickly mend your ways. As your own eye observes other people, you are in turn observed by them.

[2] Rom. 12.2   [3] Ps. 36.3

It is so pleasant and delightful to see brothers who are fervent and devout, obedient and disciplined! But it is a sad and unhappy thing to see them living disorderly lives and not practising the things to which they were called. It is very harmful to neglect the purpose of your vocation and to let your interests stray to things which are not entrusted to you.

Be mindful of the purpose you have embraced, and keep before you the image of the crucified one. You will have good cause for shame if you look at the life of Jesus Christ, because you have not yet shown much eagerness to mould yourself in his likeness, although you have for long enough been on the road of God.

A religious who meditates devoutly and intently on the most holy life and passion of the Lord will find there in abundance all that is useful and necessary for him, and there is no need for him to look outside Jesus for anything better. If only the crucified Jesus were to come into our hearts, how completely and how quickly we should be instructed!

The earnest religious submits to all the commands laid upon him and takes them well. The careless, lukewarm religious meets one trial after another and finds misery everywhere, because he is deprived of the comfort of the spirit, and is forbidden to seek it from the world. The religious who lives without discipline is preparing himself for a fall; and the religious who looks for what is easy and less demanding will always be in difficulty, because he will always find something or other that he can object to.

There are many other religious who live very strictly under the discipline of the cloister. How do they behave? They go out rarely, they live detached from the world, they eat the poorest fare and wear the coarsest clothes; they work hard and talk little, they keep long watches, rise early, prolong their prayers, are often reading, and they keep themselves very strictly disciplined. Look at the Carthusians, the Cistercians, and the monks and nuns of all the various orders. Every night they leave their beds to sing the praises of God. It would be disgraceful if you were slack in such a holy work when such a multitude of religious begin to rejoice before God. If only you had nothing else to do but praise the Lord our God with your heart and voice! If only you never had any need to eat or drink or sleep, but could praise God always, and spend all your time in spiritual pursuits! You would be much happier than you are now, when you are kept a slave to the body by its various needs. If only there were none of these needs, nothing but the need to feed the soul with spiritual food. How sad it is that we taste that food so rarely!

When a man reaches a state in which he does not look to any created thing to give him comfort, then it is that God begins to taste sweet to him, and then that he is quite content, whatever happens. In that state he does not rejoice when something splendid results, and is not saddened when something disappointing occurs, but he entrusts himself entirely and in confidence to God, who is for him all in all. Before God nothing utterly perishes or dies, but all things live for him, and hasten to do his will.

Always remember your end, and remember that wasted time does not return. You will never acquire virtues unless you show care and diligence. If you begin to grow cold, you will begin to find things difficult, but if you determine to find fervour you will find great peace, and your task will be lightened by the grace of God and your love of virtue. The man who is fervent and diligent is ready for everything.

It is a harder task to resist our faults and feelings than to sweat at manual labour. The man who does not avoid small failings gradually drifts into greater ones. You will always feel joy in the evening if you have spent the day profitably. Keep watch on yourself, rouse yourself, remind yourself, and whatever happens to others, do not take your attention from yourself. Your progress will depend on the roughness you show your old nature. Amen.

BOOK 2

SOME ADVICE ON THE INNER LIFE

I

On the inner life

The kingdom of God is within you,[1] says our Lord.

Turn to the Lord with all your heart and give up this worthless world; then your soul will find rest. Learn indifference to all that lies outside you and devote yourself to the life within, and you will see the kingdom of God coming in you. The kingdom of God means finding our peace and our joy in the Holy Spirit,[2] and the worldly cannot receive it. Christ will come to you and show you his comfort if you will prepare for him a worthy house in your heart. All his loveliness and his glory he keeps for the house of the soul, and there it is that he takes his pleasure. Many are the times he comes to the man who lives the inward life, and to him he grants sweet conversation, glad comfort, great peace and amazing friendship.

O faithful soul! Prepare your heart for this bridegroom, so that he may be willing to come to you and dwell within you. For he says, *If a man has any love for me, he will be true to my word . . . and we will both come to him, and make our continual abode with him.*[3]

Make room for Christ then, and deny entrance to all others. When you have Christ, you are rich and have all you require; he himself will faithfully provide for you and supply you with everything, so that you have no need to look to men. Men soon change and it is not long before they fail you; but Christ abides

[1] Luke 17.21   [2] Rom. 14.17   [3] John 14.23

for ever, and stands by you immovably, right to the end. Mortal men are weak, and so you should not rely on anyone, not even a good person and one you are fond of; nor should it cause you any great distress if people sometimes resist and contradict you—those who are with you today can oppose you tomorrow; they swing right round like the wind.

Rest your whole confidence on God, and let him be your fear and your love. He will reply on your behalf and in his wisdom do what is best for you. You *have an everlasting city, but not here;*[4] wherever you go you are a stranger and an exile, nor will you ever find rest unless you are one with Christ in your heart. Why do you look round about you here, when this is not the place where you are meant to find your rest? Your home should be in heavenly places, and you should be looking on all earthly things as transient. All things pass away, and you are passing with them. Take care not to cling to them, or you may be entangled and perish. Let the most high God take care of you,[5] and see that your prayers are directed Christwards without ceasing.

If you are not able to contemplate high and heavenly things, rest in the Passion of Christ, and be content to dwell within his sacred wounds. If you resort with devotion to the wounds and precious scars of Jesus, you will find great comfort in trouble. You will not mind so much if men despise you, and you will find it easy to bear when they speak against you. Christ too was despised by men in this world, and in his greatest need was abandoned by friends and followers and left to face humiliation. Christ was prepared to suffer and to be despised. Dare you raise any complaint? Christ had enemies and detractors. Do you expect to find

[4] Hebr. 13.14   [5] Wis. 5.16

everyone a friend and benefactor? How can you be
rewarded for endurance if you have never met anything
that has to be endured? If you are not prepared to
suffer opposition, how can you be the friend of Christ?
You must endure with Christ and for the sake of Christ,
if you wish to reign with Christ.

If you had once entered completely into the heart of
Jesus and had tasted just a little of his burning love,
then you would care nothing about your own convenience or inconvenience. Instead you would rejoice
when insult was offered you—for the love of Jesus
makes a man unmindful of himself.

A man who loves Jesus and the truth, who is delivered from undisciplined desires and really lives the
inward life, can turn to God with nothing to hold him
back. In spirit he can rise beyond himself and rest in
peace and joy.

When a man can value all things as they really are
and not as they are said or thought to be, then he is
really wise and taught by God, not men.[6]

The man who knows how to walk the road of the
inward life and set little store by things outside himself,
has no need of special places nor set times to perform
his exercises of devotion. The man who is living the
inward life can soon still all his thoughts, because he
never abandons himself entirely to outward things. No
physical toil is any obstacle to him, nor any activity
that must be performed—he can adjust himself to anything that comes. The man whose inner life is well-
ordered and disciplined does not care about men's per-
verse strange ways; for a man is only hindered and distracted from God in so far as he involves himself in
what goes on around him.

If you were in a good state and thoroughly purified,

[6] St Bernard, *Sermons* (*de diversis* 18,1 *Migne* 183, col.
587)

everything would help to secure your good and contribute to your progress. The reason why you are so often angry and upset is because you are not yet completely dead to your own interests and separated from all that is earthly. There is nothing that pollutes and entangles the human heart so much as an unpurged love for things that have been created. Only if you refuse outward comforts will you be able to glimpse the things of heaven and often know the inward joy.

II

On submitting humbly

You are not to mind greatly who is for you or against you, but take good care that God is with you in everything you do. Make sure you have a good conscience, and God will watch over you—and if God is prepared to support a man, no one else's unpleasantness can hurt him. If you know how to suffer in silence, you will undoubtedly find the Lord delivering you. He knows the time and the method by which he will save you, and so you should leave yourself to him; it is God's nature to help and to rescue from humiliation of every kind.

It is often a great help to us in maintaining our humility if others are aware of our failings and point them out. If a man humbles himself when he has done wrong, he soon wins others over, and appeases those who are angry with him.

It is the humble man whom God protects and delivers, the humble whom he loves and comforts. It is to the humble that he turns a willing ear and grants his grace in abundance; and after he has been downtrodden he lifts him up to glory. It is to the humble that he reveals his secrets, and he lovingly draws him and calls him to him. If a humble man is humiliated

his peace is not disturbed, because he does not live by
the world—his life depends on God.

Only when you think yourself of less importance
than everybody else may you consider that you have
made some progress.

III

On the good man who spreads peace

Live in peace yourself and then you can bring peace to
others—a peaceable man does more good than a learned
one. A man who is prey to strong emotions turns even
what is good to evil, and is ready to believe evil, whereas
the good peaceable man turns everything to good. A man
who lives in peace does not suspect anyone; but a
discontented, unsettled man is tormented by all kinds
of suspicions. He is not quiet himself, and he does not
allow others to be quiet. He often says what he should
not and neglects to do what he should; he is aware of
others' obligations but fails to observe his own.

Turn your indignation on yourself in the first place;
then you can with some justice turn it on your neighbour. You are skilled in finding excuses and in putting
a good complexion on your own actions, and yet you
are unwilling to listen to the excuses of others. It would
be more reasonable to accuse yourself and excuse your
brother. If you want others to bear with you, you
must bear with others.

See how far you are still from the true love and
humility that does not know how to be angry or
offended with anyone, except itself. It is no great
achievement to be able to live with good, gentle people
—everyone naturally finds that a pleasant thing. Every
one of us likes to have an easy life, and prefers people
that agree with him. But to be able to live with

unresponsive, unpleasant or undisciplined people is a sign of great grace. It deserves praise, and is a deed nobly done.

There are some people who live in peace themselves, and are also at peace with others. There are some who neither enjoy peace in their own lives, nor leave others in peace—they are a burden to other people and even more of a burden to themselves. There are others who not only keep themselves in peace but are always ready to guide others back to peace.

Yet in this wretched life of ours, peace must depend not on freedom from distress, but on the ability to submit to suffering humbly. It is the man who knows best how to endure who will preserve the deepest peace. It is this sort of man that overcomes himself and is master of the world, that is the friend of Christ and the heir of heaven.

IV

On a pure heart and a sincere purpose

There are two wings on which man soars away from earthly things—single-mindedness and purity. Single-mindedness shows itself in what we purpose, purity in what we feel. It is by single-mindedness that we reach towards God, by purity that we grasp him and taste his sweetness.

You will not find anything to hinder you in good actions when your heart is once freed from uncontrolled desires. If you intend and desire nothing but the will of God and your neighbour's good, you will know that inner freedom.

If your heart were right, then every created thing would be a mirror to life and a book of holy doctrine, for no creature is so small and mean that it cannot display God's goodness. If your heart were good and pure, there would be nothing to prevent you from looking at everything and really understanding it, for a pure heart can penetrate heaven and hell.

A man's impressions of the world depend on what he is in his heart. If there is joy in the world, the man whose heart is pure will certainly possess it. If there is trouble and distress anywhere, the bad conscience is the one more likely to feel it.

When iron is put in the furnace, it loses its rust and becomes white-hot through and through; in the same way, a man who turns wholeheartedly to God is stripped of his spiritual lethargy and is transformed into a new person.

When a man's enthusiasm cools, he shrinks from small tasks, and is ready to let in comfort from outside; but when he really begins to overcome himself and walk boldly in the way of God, then he hardly troubles about things which he found so burdensome before.

V

On turning our eyes on ourselves

We cannot rely on our own judgment, because we often lack both grace and discernment. The light within us is small, and we soon lose even that through carelessness. Besides, we often do not realize how blind we are in our hearts—we behave badly, and worse still, excuse what we have done; we feel anger, and call it righteous indignation; we censure small faults in others, and pass over worse ones in ourselves; we are quick enough to sense and brood over what we have to bear from others, but we do not notice how much they have to bear from us. Anyone who considers his own life with thoroughness and honesty has no reason to judge another harshly.

The man who lives the inward life puts the care of his own soul before all other cares. The man who is really concentrating on himself finds it easy to be silent where others are concerned. You will never achieve inwardness and devotion unless you avoid remarking on other people's business, and keep your thoughts for yourself. If you are really concentrating on yourself and God, anything that you observe outside will make little impression on you.

Where are you when your thoughts go wandering off? You have ranged over everything, but have you made any progress while you neglected yourself? If you are to have peace and real union, you must put all this aside and have nothing before your eyes but your own inner life. Your progress depends on keeping yourself free from commitment to any temporal concern; if you let your thoughts dwell on anything that belongs to the world, you will fall far short of the goal.

You should find nothing great or wonderful or lovely or pleasurable, except God only and what comes from him. Any comfort you meet from created objects consider utterly worthless, for a soul that truly loves God disregards all else, as it all falls short of him. It is God the eternal, the immeasurable, the filler of all things, who alone can solace the soul and bring true joy to the heart.

VI

On the gladness of a good conscience

The glory of a good man is the witness of a good conscience. Have a good conscience, and you will always have gladness; for a good conscience is able to endure a great deal, and be glad even in adversity, whereas a bad conscience is always fearful and restless. You will enjoy quiet rest if conscience does not condemn you.[1]

Only when you have done well should you feel glad. The wicked never have true happiness, and do not know peace in their hearts, because *for the rebellious, the Lord says, there is no peace.*[2] Do not believe them if they say, 'Look how prosperous we are. How can harm befall us?[3] Who will dare attack us?'—God's anger will suddenly rise up against them, what they have done will be utterly destroyed and all their designs come to nothing.[4]

It is not hard for the lover of Christ to glory *even over afflictions,*[5] and this kind of glorying is glorying in the cross of the Lord.[6] The glory that men give and receive never lasts for long, for the glorying of this world is always linked with sorrow.

The glory of good men lies in their conscience, not in what people say of them. The gladness of the upright comes from God and depends on him; their joy comes from the truth. A man who desires the true eternal glory has no interest in the glory of this world; but anyone who looks for this world's glory and in his secret heart does not despise it, is shown to have but little love for the heavenly glory.

[1] I John 3.21   [2] Is. 48.22; 57.21
[3] Mic. 3.11   [4] Ps. 145.4
[5] Rom. 5.3   [6] Gal. 6.14

A man who cares nothing for praise or blame knows great inward peace, and it is easy for the man whose conscience is clean to find contentment and quiet. Praise does not make you holier than you are, nor blame more wicked. You are exactly what you are— you cannot be said to be any better than you are in the eyes of God. If you are attending to what you really are within you, you will not care what men are saying of you. Man looks at the outside, but God looks at the heart; man weighs actions, but God probes intentions.

If a man always does well and yet sets no great store by himself it is a sign that his heart is humble. If he has no desire to find comfort in any created thing, it is a sign of great purity and of inward confidence. If he feels no need of men's support and assurance, it is clear that he has committed himself entirely to God. For as the blessed Paul says, *It is the man whom God accredits, not the man who takes credit to himself, that proves himself to be true metal.*[7]

It is the mark of the inward-living man to break all ties of affection with the outside world, and to walk with God in his heart.

VII

On loving Jesus above all things

If a man knows what it is to love Jesus, and to disregard himself for the sake of Jesus, then he is really blessed. We have to abandon all we love for the one we love, for Jesus wants us to love him only above all other things. The love of creatures is fickle and unreliable, but the love of Jesus is trustworthy and enduring. The man who clings to created things will fall

[7] II Cor. 10.18

with them when they fall, but a man who embraces
Jesus will be upheld for ever.

It is Jesus whom you must love and keep to be your
friend; when all else fades away, he will not leave you,
nor let you perish at the end. Whether you will or no,
you must one day leave everything behind. Keep yourself close to Jesus in life as well as death; commit yourself to his faithfulness, for he only can help you when
everything else will fail.

Your Beloved is not one to let a rival in; he wants to
have your heart to himself, and to rule there like a king
on the throne that is his right. If you knew how to
empty your house of created things, then Jesus would
be glad to dwell with you.

Anything you give to the world and not to Jesus, you
will find almost a total loss. Do not lean on the reed
that bends with the wind, and do not trust it—*all
mortal things are like grass, and all their glory like the
bloom of grass that falls.*[1] If you only look at the outward appearance of men you will soon be disappointed,
for if you expect other people to bring you comfort
and advantage, you are more likely to meet with loss.
If you look for Jesus in everything, it will be Jesus that
you find; if you look for yourself, you will find yourself,
and it will lead to your destruction. A man who fails
to look for Jesus does himself more harm than the whole
world and all his enemies can.

[1] I Peter 1.24-5; *v.* also Is. 40.6-7

VIII

On close friendship with Jesus

When Jesus is with us, all is well and nothing seems difficult; but when Jesus is not with us, everything is hard. When Jesus is not speaking in our hearts comfort means nothing, but if Jesus speaks just one word we experience abundant comfort. Remember how Mary Magdalene rose at once from the place where she sat weeping when Martha said to her, *The Master is here and bids thee come.*[1] It is a blessed moment when Jesus calls us from tears to the joy of the spirit.

How unmoved and hard you are without Jesus; how foolish and empty if you desire anything but him. Surely this is a greater loss than the loss of the whole world? What can the world give you without Jesus? To be without Jesus is a bitter hell, but to be with him is sweet paradise. If Jesus is with you, no enemy can harm you. The man who finds Jesus finds a wonderful treasure, a treasure beyond all other treasure. The man who loses Jesus loses a great possession, greater than all the world. The man who lives without Jesus is in direst poverty, but the man who is close to Jesus has abundant riches.

It is a great art to know how to keep company with Jesus, and great wisdom to know how to hold him. If you are humble and peaceable, Jesus will be with you. Be devout and quiet, and Jesus will stay with you.

It is easy to drive Jesus away and lose his grace, if you turn away from him to outward things. And if you drive him away and lose him, whom will you turn to then? whom will you choose to be your friend? You

[1] John 11.28

cannot live happily without a friend—and if Jesus is not your friend beyond all others, you will find yourself very sad and lonely. You are a fool if you find your confidence and joy in any other. You must choose to have the whole world against you rather than Jesus offended at you. Of all you hold dear, let Jesus only be your especial love.

You must love all people for the sake of Jesus, but you must love Jesus for himself; and Jesus Christ is the only person who may be loved beyond all others, for he alone is good and faithful, beyond all other friends. For Jesus' sake, and in Jesus, you must value enemies as well as friends, and you must pray to him for all of them, so that all may learn to know and love him.

You must never desire any unique love or praise for yourself, for that belongs to God alone who has no other like him. You must never wish to be the centre of anyone else's thoughts, nor should you let your own thoughts and affections be centred on somebody else— Jesus must be in you and in every good man.

See that you are inwardly free and purified, unattached to any created thing. You must be stripped of everything and must bring to God a heart that is pure, if you wish to be free and see how gracious the Lord is. And you will certainly not be able to do this unless his grace goes before and leads you on, enabling you to dismiss all others and send them right away, and then when you are left alone, be joined to God alone. For when the grace of God comes to a man, he finds himself able to do all things; but when it leaves him, he is poor and weak, and abandoned to the lash of misery. At such times he must not give way to depression or despair, but wait calmly for the will of God, and bear all that happens to him so that Jesus Christ is praised. For after winter comes summer, after night comes day, after the storm great calm.

IX

On doing without comfort

It is not difficult to despise the comfort that comes from
men when we have comfort from God, but it is a very
great thing to bear the absence not only of human comfort but of God's as well. It is a great thing if, to do
God honour, we are willing for our hearts to suffer
exile; if we are prepared not to seek our own satisfaction in anything, nor to think about what we have
earned.

Is there anything remarkable in feeling joy and
devotion when grace comes to you? Everyone longs
for such a moment. A man who is borne along by the
grace of God rides pleasantly enough, and it is no
wonder if he feels no burden when he is carried by the
Almighty and led by the great Guide.

We like to have something to comfort us, and man
finds it hard to throw off his natural self. Yet the holy
martyr Laurence overcame the world together with his
priest, since he paid no attention to what seemed delightful in this life, and for love of Christ, quietly accepted the loss of Sixtus, God's high priest, whom he
loved very much. In this way he overcame love of man
by love of the Creator, and instead of the comfort he
had in man he preferred the will of God. You too
must learn to leave a dear and beloved friend for the
love of God, and not resent it when your friend leaves
you, but remember that all of us must one day be parted
from one another.

There is a long hard struggle in the heart of man
before he learns to overcome himself completely and
transfer all his affections to God. When a man depends on himself, it is easy for him to fall away to

human comfort, but the man who really loves Christ and earnestly strives towards virtue does not fall back on such comforts. He does not desire the pleasant sensations that this life affords, but prefers strict exercises and enduring hard toil for Christ.

When the comfort of the spirit is given you from God, receive it with thanks; but realize that it is a gift from God, not something you deserve. Do not feel pride or excessive joy or empty presumption, but feel more humble at the gift; and be more cautious and guarded in all you do, because this hour will pass and temptation will follow. When comfort is taken away from you, do not immediately fall into despair, but humbly and patiently wait for the merciful gift of heaven, for God is able to restore your comfort, giving you more than before.

This is nothing new or strange to those who have experienced the way of God, for the great saints and the prophets of long ago often knew this sort of alteration. So we find one of them saying of the time when grace was with him, *I too had thought in time of ease, nothing can shake me now.*[1] But then grace was withdrawn and he tells us what he suffered: *Then thou didst turn thy face away from me, and I was at peace no more.*[2] Yet he did not despair, but prayed to the Lord more urgently, and said, *Lord, I was fain to plead with thee, cry upon God for pity.*[3] *Listen, Lord, and spare; Lord, let thy aid befriend me.*[4] At last he received the reward of his prayer, and he proclaims that God had heard him, and tells how he replied: *With that thou didst turn my sadness into rejoicing; thou hast . . . girded me about with gladness.*[5]

If God dealt like this with the great saints, we who are weak and poor must not despair if sometimes we feel fervour and sometimes we are cold, for the Spirit

[1-5] Ps. 29. 7, 8, 9, 11, 12

comes and goes according to his own good pleasure.
As the blessed Job says, *Never a day dawns but thou
wilt surprise him at his post; never a moment when
thou art not making proof of him.*[6]

So I cannot rest my hopes or put my trust in anything except the great mercy of God and the hope of
heavenly grace. Even if I have around me good men,
devout brethren, faithful friends, holy books, fine treatises, sweet chants and hymns, all these are of little help
and give little pleasure when I am abandoned by grace
and left to my own poverty. Then there is no better
remedy than patience and self-denial in the will of God.
I have never found anyone so religious and devout
that he did not sometimes feel grace withdrawn and his
fervour lessened. There has never been any saint so
caught up to heaven and illumined that he was not
tempted either before or after. For no man is worthy
of the sublime contemplation of God unless for God's
sake he has been exercised by some trial. Temptation is
often the sign of comfort to come, for it is to those
who have been tried in temptation that the comfort of
heaven is promised. *Who wins the victory?* he says. *I
will give him fruit from the tree of life.*[7] On the other
hand, the divine comfort is given to a man to make him
stronger to bear adversity, and it will be followed by
temptation so that the good gift does not make him
proud. The Devil does not go to sleep, and the old
nature is not yet dead. Therefore you must not cease
to prepare yourself for battle, for an enemy who never
rests surrounds you to right and to left.

[6] Job 7.18   [7] Apoc. 2.7

X

On gratitude for the grace of God

Why do you expect rest when you were born for toil? Prepare yourself for hardship, not for happiness, for bearing the cross, not for being glad.

Even worldly people would be glad to receive comfort and spiritual joy if they could keep them always, for the comforts of the spirit surpass all the delights of the world and the pleasures of the body. All the delights of this world are unsatisfactory or shameful, but the delights of the spirit alone are lovely and good. They are born of virtues and are poured by God into hearts that are pure. But no man is able to enjoy the comfort that comes from God all the time and as he pleases, because the time of temptation never comes to an end.

What does hinder the merciful gift from heaven is over-confidence and false liberty of mind. God does well in giving us the grace of comfort, but man does ill in not giving it all back to him with thanks. The gifts of grace cannot flow in our hearts, because we are ungrateful to the giver, and do not pour them back into the fount from which they came. For grace can only be given to the man who has grace to give thanks, and the gift which is given to the humble will be taken from the proud.

I would rather not have comfort if it takes away compunction, nor have I any desire for contemplation if it leads to pride. Not everything that is high is holy, nor is everything that is pleasant good; not every desire we have is pure, nor is all that we hold dear acceptable to God. The grace I am glad to receive is one which makes me more humble and careful, more ready to renounce myself.

Grace is given to a man to teach him, and is taken away to train him; and anyone who has experienced this will not venture to attribute any good thing to himself, but will acknowledge his poverty and nakedness instead. Give to God what is God's, and assign to yourself what is yours—that is, attribute all grace to God with thanks, and take to yourself all the guilt, acknowledging that there is a penalty that should be paid for your guilt.

Put yourself always in the lowest place, and you will be given the highest—without the lowest the highest cannot exist. The greatest saints in the sight of God are the least in their own eyes. The more glorious they are, the greater the humility they feel. Full of truth and heavenly glory, they have no desire for groundless glorying. They are founded and fixed in God, and cannot be shaken by pride. They ascribe to God whatever good they have received, and are not ambitious for honour from one another, but desire the honour that comes from him who alone is God.[1] Their aim is the praise of God above all things in themselves and in all the saints, and they are always seeking this end.

Show yourself grateful therefore for the smallest gift, and you will be worthy of receiving greater ones. Let the smallest be in your eyes equivalent to the greatest, and an insignificant gift the equal of a special favour. If you consider the rank of the giver, nothing that he gives will then seem small or worthless, for no gift can be small that comes from the most high God. Even if he gives punishment and scourging, we should accept it with gladness, for anything he allows to happen to us he does for our salvation always.

A man who wishes to retain the grace of God must

[1] John 5.44

show thankfulness when it is given him, and patience if it is taken away. He should pray for its return and then be careful and humble so as not to lose it.

XI

On the fewness of those who love the cross of Jesus

Jesus has in these days many people who love his heavenly kingdom, but few who bear his cross. He has many who desire comfort, but few who are ready for trials. He has found many to share his table, but few to share his fast. Everyone longs to rejoice with him, but few are ready to suffer for him. Many follow Jesus as far as the breaking of the bread, but few go so far as to drink the cup of his passion. Many glory in his miracles, few follow him in the shame of the cross. Many people love Jesus as long as misfortune does not fall on them; they praise him and bless him as long as they are receiving any comfort from him, but if Jesus hides himself or leaves them for a while, they complain bitterly or fall into great despair.

Yet those who love Jesus for his own sake and not for any comfort they can get from him, bless him in every trial and distress of heart, just as they do amidst the richest spiritual comfort. Even if he were never prepared to grant them comfort, they would still be always praising him and always wanting to offer him thanks. What power there is in pure love for Jesus, unmixed with any self-seeking or thought of personal gain!

Surely 'mercenary' is the right name for the people who are always looking for spiritual comforts; and those who are always thinking about their own profit and advantage quite clearly love themselves, not Christ.

Where will you find a man who is prepared to serve

God for nothing? It is not often one finds anyone so spiritual that he is stripped of everything. Who can find a man who is really poor in spirit, emptied of every created thing?—such a man is *a rare treasure, brought from distant shores.*[1]

If a man gives up all that he has in the world,[2] it is still nothing. If he does great penance, it is still a small thing. If he attains all knowledge,[3] it still falls short. If he has great virtue and burning devotion, he still lacks much—the one thing in fact which he needs most of all. And that is to renounce everything, and then to renounce himself; to leave self entirely behind, and to have no vestige left of love for self. Then when he has done everything which he knows he should do, he must realize he has done nothing. If he has done anything worth-while, he must think nothing of it, but honestly declare himself a worthless servant. As he who is the Truth says, *When you have done all that was commanded you, you are to say, We are servants, and worthless.*[4] Then that man will be really poor and naked in spirit, and will be able to say with the prophet, I am *friendless and forlorn.*[5] Yet the man who knows how to renounce himself and all things, and put himself in the lowest place, has more riches, power and freedom than anyone.

[1] Prov. 31.10   [2] Cant. 8.7   [3] I Cor. 13.2
[4] Luke 17.10   [5] Ps. 24.16

XII

On the royal way of the holy cross

Renounce self, take up your cross, follow Jesus.[1]

These words seem very hard, yet it will be much harder to hear those final words—*Go far from me, you that are accursed, into that eternal fire.*[2] The people who now gladly hear and obey the words which bring them the cross will have no fear then of the words that mean eternal condemnation. When the Lord comes to judge, it will be this sign of the cross that is in the heaven. Then all the servants of the cross who in this life followed in the steps of the crucified Jesus will come before Christ the Judge with confidence and boldness.

So why are you afraid to take up the cross, when it leads us to the kingdom?

In the cross is salvation, in the cross is life; in the cross is defence from enemies, in the cross heaven's sweetness is outpoured; in the cross is strength of mind, in the cross is joy of spirit; in the cross is highest virtue, in the cross is perfect holiness. There is no salvation for the soul nor hope of eternal life except in the cross. Take up your cross then, and follow Jesus, and you will enter eternal life. He went before you, carrying his cross, and on the cross he died for you, so that you too should carry your cross, and long for a death on the cross. For if you share his death, you will also share his life.[3] If you are with him in his suffering, you will be with him in his glory.

All that matters is the cross and dying on that cross —there is no other way to life and real inward peace except the way of the holy cross, and of daily dying to

[1] Matt. 16.24   [2] Matt. 25.41   [3] Rom. 6.8

self. Go where you like, look for what you like, you will not find a higher way above or a safer way below than the way of the holy cross.

Even if you arrange everything to suit your own views and wishes you will always find that you still have to suffer something, whether you want to or not—the cross will always be there. If you do not suffer physical pain, you will have inward trials of the spirit : sometimes God will abandon you, sometimes your neighbour give you something to bear, and worse still, you will often be a burden to yourself. No remedy or comfort will be able to deliver or relieve you, but you will have to bear it as long as God wills it so. For it is God's will for you to learn to endure troubles without receiving comfort, so that you will submit entirely to him, and from this trouble learn humility. No one feels the Passion of Christ in his heart as much as the man whose lot it is to suffer as he did.

So the cross is always close by and waits for you everywhere. You cannot escape it, wherever you may run; for everywhere you go you take yourself, and always you will find yourself. Look up or down, out or in, there too you will find the cross; and all the time you must go on being patient if you wish to have inward peace and to win a crown that will last for ever.

If you carry your cross with gladness, it will carry you and lead you to that longed-for goal where there will be no more suffering, though there will always be suffering here. If you carry it grudgingly, you will make it a burden and weigh yourself down, but all the same you will have to bear it. If you throw one cross aside you will certainly find another, and possibly one that is heavier to bear.

Do you think you can escape what no man on earth has been able to avoid? Did any one of the saints escape a cross and a trial while he was in this world? Not even Jesus Christ our Lord was free from the pain of his passion for one hour while he lived. *It was fitting,* he said, *that Christ should suffer and rise from the dead, and enter so into his glory.*[4] How can you look for some other way than this royal way, which is the way of the holy cross? The whole life of Christ was a cross and a martyrdom—do you expect peace and joy? You go very, very wrong if you expect to do anything but endure troubles, for all this life that we live as mortal creatures is full of sorrows and marked everywhere with crosses—and it often happens that a man finds even heavier crosses as he makes spiritual progress and begins to rise, because his growing love makes his exile harder to bear.

Yet the man who suffers all these afflictions is not without the relief of comfort, because he realizes that from bearing his cross, great profit comes to him; as long as he submits to it willingly, all the burden of his suffering is transformed into the assurance of comfort coming from God. The more his body is reduced by suffering, the more his spirit is strengthened by inward grace. His desire to be moulded to the cross of Christ makes him long for trials and difficulties; and he finds such strength in this that he would not want to be delivered from his sorrow and distress if he could, since he believes that as he bears more and heavier burdens for God's sake, so he becomes more acceptable to him.

This desire is not due to any human virtue but to the grace of Christ, which works so powerfully in man's weak body that, through the burning passion of the spirit, it comes to love and strive for the very things that naturally it hates and avoids. It is not natural for

[4] Luke 24.46 and 26.

a man to carry the cross, and to love the cross, to buffet his body and make it his slave,[5] to avoid honours and to bear insults gladly, to show no regard for himself and to expect none from others, to suffer all kinds of adversity and loss, and to have no wish for this world's prosperity. If you rely on yourself, you will find you have no power to do any of this; but if you trust in the Lord, strength will be given you from heaven, and the world and your natural self will be put under your control. You will not even fear our enemy the Devil, if you are armed with faith and signed with the cross of Christ.

Make yourself ready then like a good faithful servant of Christ manfully to carry the cross of your Lord, who was crucified for love of you. Prepare yourself to bear a great deal of adversity and all kinds of discomfort in this unhappy life, because it will be the same wherever you are, and you will find it so wherever you hide yourself. It is right for it to be like this, and there is no way of escaping sorrow and the trouble that evil brings—you have to endure what human nature involves. Drink the cup of the Lord with love, if you want to be his friend and have any share with him. Leave the question of spiritual comfort to God—let him do as he wills with it. Make up your mind to bear your troubles; consider them in fact the greatest comforts, for even if you alone could undergo every suffering there is,[6] *these present sufferings* are not to be counted *as the measure of that glory,*[7] nor are they enough to win it.

When you reach a state in which troubles become sweet and satisfying to you for Christ's sake, then you may think that all is well with you, because you have found paradise on earth. As long as you find suffering a

[5] I Cor. 9.27
[6] St Bernard, *Sermons (I in festo annunt. B.M.V.* Migne 183, col. 383)   [7] Rom. 8.18

burden and try to escape it, things will go badly with
you, and you will always be running away from trouble;
but if you once accept that suffering and the killing of
the old nature are what you have to face, your state will
soon improve and you will know peace.

Even if you are carried up to the third heaven with
Paul,[8] that will not mean you are secured from all
adversity—*I have yet to tell him,* says Jesus, *how much
suffering he will have to undergo for my name's sake.*[9]
So suffering lies ahead of you, if it is your wish to love
Jesus and serve him continually. If only you were
really worthy of suffering something for the name of
Jesus—what glory would be waiting for you! How
all the saints of God would rejoice! How those around
you would be strengthened! For everyone praises endurance, but few are prepared to endure. You might
with good reason accept a little suffering for Christ,
when many people endure worse things for the sake of
the world.

You can be certain that the life you must lead is a
dying life, and that a man begins to live before God
only as he dies to his own nature. No one is fitted to
understand heavenly things unless he submits to bearing
adversity for Christ's sake. Nothing is more acceptable
to God, or more healthful for you in this world, than
willing suffering for Christ. If the choice were yours,
you should choose suffering and adversity for the sake
of Christ rather than comforts and spiritual refreshment. Then you would be more like Christ, and closer
to all the saints. Merit and progress in our calling are
not found in delights and comforts, but in bearing great
burdens and troubles. If there had been anything that
advanced man's salvation more than suffering, Christ
would certainly have shown it by word and deed. For
he clearly impresses on the disciples who were following

[8] II Cor. 12.2   [9] Acts 9.16

him, and on all those thinking of following him, the need to carry the cross; for he says, *If any man has a mind to come my way, let him renounce self, and take up his cross, and follow me.*[10]

So when we have read and examined everything, this must be our final conclusion—*we cannot enter the kingdom of heaven without many trials.*[11]

[10] Matt. 16.24   [11] Acts 14.21

BOOK 3

SPIRITUAL COMFORT

I

On the voice of Christ in the heart, speaking to the faithful soul

THE DISCIPLE SPEAKS : *Let me listen now to the voice of the Lord God.*[1]

Blessed is the soul that listens to the voice of the Lord and hears comforting words from him.

Blessed are the ears that catch the breath of the whisper of God, and give no heed to the whisperings of this world—blessed ears indeed, if they are listening to the Truth teaching them in their hearts and not to voices outside them.

Blessed are the eyes which are closed to all external things because they are intent upon what lies within.

Blessed are those who pierce through to that inner world and prepare themselves continually for the revelation of heaven's secrets by the way they live their daily lives. Blessed are those who long to be completely free for God, who shake off every worldly thing that could cause them hindrance.

Mark all this, my soul; bar up the doors of your senses, so that you can listen to the voice of the Lord your God. This is what your Beloved is saying : I am your salvation, your peace and your life. Keep beside me, and you will find peace. Abandon all the things that pass away, and seek the things that are eternal; for temporal things do nothing but lead you astray,

[1] Ps. 84.9

and there is no profit in the whole creation if the Creator deserts you.

Renounce all things therefore; return in faith to your Creator, and make yourself acceptable to him. Only so can you know true blessedness.

II

Truth speaks to the heart without need of words

THE DISCIPLE: *Speak on, Lord; thy servant is listening.*[1] *Perfect in thy own servant's heart the knowledge of thy will.*[2]

Do not let me turn a deaf ear to the words you utter[3] —let your warnings *soak in like the dew.*[4]

The children of Israel once said to Moses: *Do thou tell us the message; we are ready to obey thee. Do not let us hear the Lord speaking; it will cost us our lives.*[5] O Lord, my prayer is not like theirs, but with humble longing I pray with the prophet Samuel: *Speak on, Lord; thy servant is listening.* I do not want to hear Moses speaking, or any of the prophets—Lord God, speak to me yourself. You inspired and enlightened the prophets, and you alone without them can teach me perfectly. They without you cannot help me at all.

Prophets may employ words, but they do not give the spirit. They may speak with eloquence, but if you are silent they do not stir the heart. They record the message, but you make plain what it means. They show us mysteries, but you reveal their hidden sense. They declare your commands, but you give power to obey. They point out the road, but you give strength for the journey. They act on our outward senses, but you

[1] I Kings 3.10   [2] Ps. 118.125   [3] Ps. 77.1
[4] Deut. 32.2   [5] Ex. 20.19

instruct and enlighten the heart. They water the ground, but you make the soil productive. They may speak the actual words, but it is through you that we understand them.

So I do not want Moses to speak to me, but you, Lord God, the eternal Truth; for I am afraid that I shall wither away and bear no fruit, if the warning falls on my ears with no spark of response in my heart. I do not want to be judged for hearing your word and not obeying it, for knowing it and not loving it, for believing it and not observing it. *Speak on therefore, Lord; thy servant is listening. Thy words are the words of eternal life.*[6] Speak on, so that my soul may receive some comfort and my whole life be improved; speak on, so that praise and glory and everlasting honour may be brought to you.

III

We should humbly listen to what God has to say, yet many pay no attention to it

THE VOICE OF THE LORD : My son, hear what I have to say, for my words are sweet and surpass the knowledge of all the philosophers and wise men of this world. The words I speak are spirit and life,[1] and are not to be judged by human understanding. You must not turn them to fit your empty complacency, but hear them in silence, and receive them with humility and longing.

THE DISCIPLE : *Happy, Lord, is the man whom thou dost chasten, reading him the lesson of thy law. For him thou wilt lighten the time of adversity,*[2] and not leave him alone on the earth.

[6] John 6.69   [1] John 6.64   [2] Ps. 93.12-13

THE LORD : I gave my message to the prophets at the very beginning, and even now I am speaking still to all men, though many of them are hardened and do not hear my voice. There are many people who are more ready to listen to the world than God, more likely to satisfy their natural cravings than do what pleases God.

What the world promises is impermanent and of little value, and yet men are eager to serve it. I offer what is precious and lasting, and men's hearts remain unstirred. Does anyone serve and obey me with the wholehearted enthusiasm that is given to the world and its lords? *Poor Sidon, by false hopes betrayed! a cry comes up from the sea.*[3] And that cry comes up because there are people who will run a long way for an appointment with a little income attached, but to get eternal life they will hardly stir one foot from the ground. They are always on the watch for sordid money, and quarrel shamefully over a penny. It is a disgraceful thing that they are not afraid of wearing themselves out night and day for some worthless object, some small hope of gain; but for the possession that cannot be lost, for the priceless reward, for the highest honour, the endless glory, they find it a nuisance to exert themselves at all. And so you lazy, grumbling servant, you should blush to think that those people are more eager for destruction than you are for life, more pleased with shadows than you are with the truth!

The hopes of those people often disappoint them, but my promise fails no one, and never sends away empty-handed the man who trusts in me. What I have promised, I will give; what I have said, I will fulfil, if a man will only remain faithful to the end in his love for me. I am one that rewards all good men, the true Judge of all the devout.

Write my words in your heart, and study them care-

[3] Is. 23.4

fully. In time of temptation you will find them very
necessary. What you do not understand when you read
it, you will recognize when the time comes for me to
visit you. There are two ways in which I visit my
chosen ones, in temptation and in comfort; and every
day I read to them two lessons, one rebuking their
faults, the other inspiring them to grow in goodness.

Anyone who has my word and makes it of no account
has a judge appointed to try him at the last day.[4]

A prayer for the grace of devotion

O Lord my God, all my good is found in you. Who am
I, that I dare to speak to you? I am your most
wretched slave, an abject worm, much poorer and more
despicable than I know or dare to say. Yet Lord,
remember that I am nothing, have nothing, can do
nothing. You alone are good and just and holy. You
can do all things; you bestow all things and fill all
things, leaving only the sinner empty. Do not forget
your pity;[5] fill my heart with your grace, since you do
not wish what you have made to be left empty. How
can I endure myself in this unhappy life, unless you
strengthen me with your mercy and your grace? Do not
turn your face away from me, do not prolong the time
of testing; do not take your comfort from me, or my
soul will lie before you *like a land parched with
drought.*[6] Teach me, Lord, to do your will,[7] teach me
to live humbly and worthily before you—for you are
my wisdom; you know me utterly, and knew me before
the world was made and before I was born in the
world.

[4] John 12.48   [5] Ps. 24.6   [6-7] Ps. 142.6, 10

IV

We must live in God's sight in truth and humility

THE VOICE OF THE LORD: My son, tread my paths in truth, and with sincere heart aspire to me always.[1] The man who treads my paths in truth will be kept safe from the assaults of evil, and the truth will free him from those who would lead him astray, and from the sneers of the wicked. If the truth sets you free you will have freedom in earnest,[2] and you will not care about the worthless words of men.

THE DISCIPLE: Lord, that is true. Let it be so in my case. Let your truth teach me and guard me and preserve me to salvation at the end. Let it free me from all evil desires, all uncontrolled affection, and so my heart will be really free, and I will walk with you.

I will teach you what is right, says the Truth, and what is pleasing to me.

Think over your sins with sorrow and dissatisfaction, and never imagine yourself to be anything because you have done something good. You are a sinner, a prey to all kinds of emotions, unable to shake yourself free. Left to yourself, you always tend to nothingness; you soon fall, you are soon defeated, soon lose your peace and harmony. You have nothing to be proud of, but much to make you loathe yourself; you are very weak, far weaker in fact than you are able to realize.

So nothing should seem great to you of anything you do. Nothing should seem fine or precious or wonderful,

[1] Wisdom 1.1   [2] John 8.32 and 36

nothing worthy of fame, nothing magnificent, nothing really praiseworthy or desirable, but only the things that are eternal. Above all things find your happiness in the eternal Truth, at all times find sorrow in your utter worthlessness. There is nothing you should fear and hate and avoid as much as your own faults and sins, and they should cause you more distress than any material loss.

There are some who tread my paths, but not straightforwardly. Arrogance and curiosity make them want to find out my secrets and to know the deep mysteries of God, while they give no thought to their souls and their salvation. This arrogance and curiosity leads them into great temptation and sin, for I have set myself against them. You must fear the judgments of God, and tremble at the wrath of the Almighty. Do not pry into the works of the Most High, but look into your sins instead—look at the wrongs you have done, and the chances for good you have missed.

The devotion of some people lies in nothing more than books or pictures, or outward symbols and signs. Others have my name on their lips but have little of me in their hearts.

But there are others who have had their minds enlightened and their affections purified. These people are always thirsting for the things of eternity; they hate to hear of earthly things, and it is a grief to them to have to attend to the needs of the body. They know what the Spirit of truth says in their hearts, for he teaches them to scorn earthly things and to love the things of heaven. He teaches them to disregard the world and to long for heaven every moment of night and day.

V

On the wonderful effect of divine love

THE DISCIPLE : Heavenly Father and Father of my
Lord Jesus Christ, I bless you because you have in your
mercy remembered so poor a creature as me. O merciful Father, the God who gives all encouragement![1] I
bring you my thanks because you send your comfort
to encourage me when I deserve no comfort at all. O
Father with the only-begotten Son and the Holy Spirit
the Comforter, I bless you always and give you the
glory for ever.

Dear Lord and God! O Holy One, O Lover of my
soul! when you come to my heart, all that is within me
will leap up for joy. You are my glory, the rejoicing
of my heart. You are my hope and *my refuge in my
hour of peril.*[2]

Yet I am still weak in love, imperfect in goodness,
and I need your strength and comfort. So visit me often
and teach me by your holy discipline; free me from
evil passions, and cure my heart of all its undisciplined
emotions; then I shall be healthy and clean within,
made fit for loving, strong for suffering, steadfast for
enduring.

Love is a great thing, an altogether good gift, the
only thing that makes burdens light and bears all that
is hard with ease. It carries a weight without feeling it,
and makes all that is bitter sweet and pleasant to the
taste. The love of Jesus is noble and impels us to do great
things; it continually stirs us up to desire the next
stage in perfection. Love longs to be in the high places,

---

[1] II Cor. 1.3   [2] Ps. 58.17

not held down by anything base. Love longs to be free, cut loose from every earthly affection, so that the eyes of the soul may not be dimmed, so that no temporal advantage may entangle it and no obstacle cause it to fall.

Nothing is sweeter than love, nothing stronger, nothing higher, nothing broader; nothing is more lovely, nothing richer, nothing better in heaven or in earth. Love is born of God and it cannot rest anywhere but in God, beyond all created things. One who loves is borne on wings; he runs, and is filled with joy; he is free and unrestricted. He gives all to receive all, and he has all in all; for beyond all things he rests in the one highest thing, from whom streams all that is good. He does not consider the gift, but beyond all good things he turns himself to the giver.

Love often knows no measure, but burns white-hot beyond all measure. Love feels no burden, and counts up no toil; it aspires to do more than its strength allows; it does not plead impossibility, but considers it may do and can do all things. So it finds strength for anything; it completes and carries through great tasks where one who does not love would fail and fall. Love is vigilant, it sleeps without losing control; it is wearied without exhaustion, cramped without being crushed, alarmed without being destroyed. Like a living flame or a burning torch, it leaps up and safely passes through all. When a man loves, he knows the meaning of that cry that sounds in the ears of God[3] from the burning love of the soul : My God, it cries, my love ! You are wholly mine, and I am wholly yours !

Expand my heart with love, so that the lips of my soul may taste how sweet it is to love, to melt in love and float upon a sea of love. Let me be gripped by

[3] St Bernard, *Sermon*s (in psalm. *qui habitat* 17, Migne 183, col. 247)

love as I rise in adoration and wonder beyond the limits of my being. Let the song of love be on my lips as I follow my Love to the heights; let my soul, triumphant with love, faint in intensity of worship. May I love you more than myself, and myself only because of you; and in you let me love all those who truly love you. The law of love that shines from you gives us this command.

Love is eager, sincere and kind; it is glad and lovely; it is strong, patient and faithful; wise, long-suffering and resolute; and it never seeks its own ends, for where a man seeks his own ends, he at once falls out of love. Love is sensible, humble, honourable; it is not self-indulgent, thoughtless, set on foolish things, but is sober, chaste, steadfast, quiet, and guarded in every sense. Love is submissive, and obeys those set over it; for itself it has only disregard and contempt, but it is full of devotion and gratitude to God; and it goes on trusting and hoping in God even when he is no longer sweet to it, for one cannot live in love without pain. Anyone who is not prepared to endure everything and to stand by the will of the Beloved is not worthy of the name of lover. A lover must gladly accept what is hard and bitter for the sake of the Beloved, and he must not have his allegiance shaken if hardships come his way.

VI

The test of the true lover

THE VOICE OF THE LORD : My son, you are not yet a wise and determined lover.

THE DISCIPLE : Why not, Lord?

THE LORD : Because it only takes some slight adversity

to make you abandon what you are doing and start longing for some comfort. A determined lover stands firm in temptation, and does not believe the Enemy's cunning suggestions. He is content with me in prosperity, and in adversity he is contented just the same.

A wise lover does not look at the gift of the one who loves him, but at the love of the giver. He weighs the affection and not the value; and he thinks more of the Beloved than of what the Beloved has to give. The generous lover does not find his satisfaction in what I have to give, but beyond all my gifts, in me.

Still, all is not lost if you sometimes find yourself harbouring thoughts about me and my saints that are not all you would like. That good and delightful affection you sometimes feel is the result of the presence of grace, and is a foretaste of the heavenly country. You must not depend on it too much, because it comes and goes. The real sign of goodness and great merit is to resist the evil inclinations of the mind and to spurn the hints of the Devil.

You must not be alarmed by these alien thoughts, whatever gives rise to them. Keep your resolve unshaken and your purpose centred on God. It is no illusion that you are sometimes caught up in ecstasy, though you relapse immediately into your usual foolish thoughts. You are subject to these against your will, not actively creating them, and as long as you loathe them and resist them, the result is merit and not destruction.

You must realize that your ancient enemy is striving in every way to disturb the good state of your desires, and to turn you against every exercise of devotion—against reverence for the saints, against holy recollection of my passion, against profitable remembrance of your sins, against vigilance over your own heart and a firm resolve to make progress in goodness. He supplies many evil thoughts to make you feel restlessness and revulsion, to keep you back from prayer and reading holy books. He has no liking for humble confession, and if he could, he would see that you stopped making your Communion.

You must not believe him, or pay any attention to him, even though he sets his snares of deception so often in your path. When he insinuates evil, unclean thoughts, throw them back in his face. Say to him: Leave me, you foul spirit. Shame on you, you wretched unclean creature, whispering such things in my ears. Leave me alone, you evil tempter; you shall not have any power over me; Jesus shall stand at my side, a strong champion, and you shall be disappointed of your hopes![1] I would rather die and suffer every kind of punishment than say 'yes' to you. Hold your tongue, not another word. I will not listen to you any longer, however much you annoy me. *The Lord is my light and my deliverance; whom have I to fear? Though a whole host were arrayed against me, my heart would be undaunted.*[2] The Lord is *my defender, my redeemer!*[3]

Fight like a good soldier, and if you sometimes fall from weakness, gather stronger forces, trusting that I will send you richer supplies of grace. Yet beware all the time of groundless complacency and pride. It is this that leads many into error, and sometimes into blindness that can hardly be cured. You must learn caution and perpetual humility from the ruin that comes upon the proud who are foolish enough to take too much upon them.

[1] Jer. 20.11   [2] Ps. 26.1 and 3   [3] Ps. 18.15

On concealing the gift of grace under the guard of humility

THE VOICE OF THE LORD : My son, it is better and safer for you to hide away the gracious gift of devotion and not be proud of it or talk and think a great deal about it. Instead you must have an even humbler opinion of yourself, and regard the gift with caution, feeling that you are unworthy of it.

You should not let yourself be carried away by this feeling of love and devotion, which can so quickly turn into quite a different feeling. When grace has been given you, you should be reminding yourself how wretched and resourceless you are when it is taken away.

Progress in the spiritual life is made not so much when you have the gracious gift of spiritual comfort, but when you can bear its removal with humility, self-denial and patience, not letting yourself grow slack in zeal for prayer, or giving up all the other things which are your normal practice. It is good if at such times you gladly do all you can to the best of your ability and understanding, and do not let your powerlessness and spiritual distress make you abandon all interest in your inner self. There are many people who become impatient and careless the moment things go wrong. It is not always for man to choose his lot,[1] but God has the right to send blessings and comfort when he wishes, as much as he wishes, to whom he wishes, just as he pleases and no more.

Some people have not been careful where the gracious

[1] Jer. 10.23

gift of devotion was concerned, and have ruined themselves because they aimed at doing more than they were able. They did not pause to consider their own limited powers, but were guided by their own wishes and not by common sense. They presumed to do more than it was God's will for them to do, and so they soon lost the gift of grace. Although they built their nest among the stars,[2] they were deprived of everything and left resourceless, so that their poverty and humiliation might teach them not to fly on their own wings but to nestle under my care.[3]

Those who are still new and inexperienced in the way of the Lord may well be misled and come crashing down, if they do not let wiser people guide them. If they prefer to go their own way instead of believing people of experience, they will ruin themselves in the end, since they will not let themselves be dissuaded. It does not often happen that people who have a good conceit of themselves humbly accept guidance from others. It is better to have only a little knowledge combined with humility and small understanding, than to possess great treasures of learning combined with foolish self-satisfaction. It is better to have only a little, than to have much and grow proud.

A man does not behave very sensibly if he gives way to unrestrained delight when grace is given him, forgetting how poor he was before, and abandoning that modest fearfulness before the Lord which is afraid of losing the gift again. On the other hand, he does not show any virtue or sense if he abandons all hope the moment adversity or any sort of trouble comes his way, and falls into thoughts and feelings that show no faith in me. It is often the man who is too ready to feel secure in time of peace who becomes unnecessarily hopeless and fearful in war. If you knew how to keep yourself humble, apply moderation and discipline your

[2] Obad. 4   [3] Ps. 90.4

spirit, you would not fall so easily into danger and sin.

When you have received the spirit of ardour, it is a good plan to think what it will be like when the light goes away; and when that happens, to remind yourself that the light can return, though I have taken it away for a time to teach you caution and to glorify myself. It often does you more good to be tested like this than to have things always going the way you want them to. It is not necessarily a sign of merit if a man is often granted visions and spiritual comforts, nor if he has deep knowledge of the Scriptures, nor if he is raised to a position of authority; but merit may be assumed when a man's life is rooted in true humility and filled with divine love, when he always seeks God's honour solely and wholeheartedly, when he thinks nothing of himself, but truly disregards himself and even prefers to receive contempt and humiliation from others, rather than honour.

VIII

On thinking nothing of oneself in the sight of God

THE DISCIPLE : *Dust and ashes though I be, I have taken it upon me to speak to my Lord.*[1]

If I think that I am more than dust, I find you confronting me; my sins give evidence against me and I cannot but plead guilty. Yet if I condemn myself, utterly abase myself, abandon all self-esteem, treat myself as the dust that I am, then your grace will favour me, and your light will shine on my heart. Then all self-estimation, however slight, will be swallowed up in the abyss of my nothingness, and will perish for ever. It is there that you show me myself, what I am, what I was, what I have become. *I was all dumbness, I was*

[1] Gen. 18.27

all ignorance.[2] If I am left to myself, all is nothingness and weakness; but if you suddenly look my way, at once I am made strong, I am filled with new joy. What a wonderful thing it is that you suddenly lift me up like this and embrace me so kindly, when my own weight is always dragging me down to the depths.

It is your love that does this, the love that from pure affection surrounds my path, and comes to help me in my many needs, that keeps me safe from danger and rescues me from countless ills. For by sinfully loving myself, I lost myself, but by seeking you alone and loving you wholeheartedly I have found both myself and you, and by that love have been utterly humbled again; for you show me kindness, O my sweetest God, beyond all that I deserve, beyond all I dare ask or hope.

May all praise be yours, O God! for though I am unworthy of any good gift, yet in your generosity and infinite goodness you never cease to bless even the ungrateful and those who turn their backs on you and wander far away.

Turn us back to yourself, so that we may be thankful, humble and loving; for you are our salvation, our boldness and our strength.

IX

Everything must be referred to God, the ultimate goal

THE VOICE OF THE LORD: My son, if you desire to be really happy, you must make me your final and ultimate goal. Such a purpose will purify those affections of yours, which are too often deflected away towards yourself and the things I have created; and that harms

[2] Ps. 72.22

you, since you become dry and powerless wherever you seek yourself. So you must refer everything solely to me, for I have given you all. You must view every single thing as proceeding from the supreme Good, and for that reason bring everything back to me, and return it to its source.

From me, great and small, rich and poor, draw living water from a living spring, and those who serve me freely and gladly will receive grace answering to grace.[1] But no one can hold fast to the true joy if he makes his boast in anything outside me, or finds his delight in some good thing of his own. He will not feel his heart expanding in gladness, but he will be very conscious of oppression and contraction. So you must not attribute any good thing to yourself, or think that any man's goodness is his own, but acknowledge that all is God's, without whom man has nothing.

I gave everything, and I want everything back again. I am very strict in demanding the giving of thanks. This is the truth that puts to flight vain boasting. Once you receive real love and the grace of heaven, you will feel no grudge, no oppression of your heart; and no love of self will occupy you, for the love of God overcomes all things, and expands all the powers of the soul.

If you are truly wise you will find in me your only joy and hope, for *none is good, except God only,*[2] and he is above all things to be praised, in all things to be blessed.

[1] John 1.16   [2] Luke 18.19

X

What delight there is in spurning the whole world and becoming the servant of God

THE DISCIPLE : I will speak to my Lord again, and I will not keep silent. I will cry out so that my God may hear, my Lord, my King in the heavens : *What treasures of loving-kindness, Lord, dost thou store up for the men who fear thee.*[1]

But what for those who love you and serve you with all their heart? Truly, it is beyond man's power to tell the loving-kindness that you pour out on those who love you, when you let them see yourself. And I see the sweetness of your love in this above all things : when I did not exist, you created me; when I wandered far from you, you brought me back in order to make me your servant, and then commanded me to give you my love.

O spring of never-ceasing love, what shall I say of you? How can I forget you, when you stooped to remember me though I was sick and lost? You have treated your servant more kindly than he could ever hope, you have shown him more graciousness and friendship than he could ever deserve.

What return can I make[2] for your kindness to me? It is not everyone that is allowed to abandon all, renounce the world and take up the monastic life. Yet I should not think it a great thing to be serving you— how can it be a great thing when every creature is bound to offer you its service? This is the great and wonderful thing—that you are prepared to take such a

[1] Ps. 30.20   [2] Ps. 115.3

destitute and unworthy creature into your service, and to add him to your beloved household. Why, everything I have, everything by which I serve you, is yours already.

Yet the truth is that you serve me more than I serve you. Here around us are the heaven and the earth, which you created to be the common drudges of man,[8] and every day they fulfil the commands you gave them. More than that, you have even appointed angels to serve the needs of men. But what surpasses all is that you have stooped to serve man yourself, and have promised to give yourself to him.

What return can I make for all these countless gifts? If only I could serve you all the days of my life! If only I were able, for one day even, to offer you the service you deserve! You are worthy of all service, and all honour, and everlasting praise. Truly you are my God and I am your poor servant. I am bound to serve you with all my strength and never tire of bringing you praise. That is what I long for, what I desire—in your mercy supply what I lack.

It is a great honour and great glory to serve you, and for your sake to reject all things as worthless. For those who of their own free will submit to your holy service will receive great grace; those who reject all the delights of this physical life for love of you will find the sweet comfort of the Holy Spirit; and those who for your sake step out upon the narrow way and cease to care about anything in this world, will know great inner freedom.

What joy and delight it is to serve God like this, when it brings real holiness and freedom! What a sacred thing it is to be God's servant in an order, for that makes a man equal to the angels, acceptable to God.

[8] Deut. 4.19

fearful to devils, and commendable to all the faithful. Such a servitude is desirable, a thing to be coveted, for by it the highest good is won, and a joy attained that will endure for ever.

XI

Our inmost desires need to be examined and controlled

THE VOICE OF THE LORD: My son, there are many lessons that you have not yet taken in.

THE DISCIPLE: What are they, Lord?

THE LORD: You have to learn to bring your desires wholly into line with my will. You must be no lover of your own ends, but a man who endeavours with all his heart to do what pleases me. You are often full of enthusiasm for some scheme, but you must stop and consider whether your real motive is to honour me or bring yourself some advantage. If you are doing it for me, you will be content whatever I decree; but if there is any suggestion of personal gain, you will find yourself burdened and hindered. So take care not to throw yourself wholeheartedly into any scheme until you have first consulted me, or later on you may find yourself regretting and hating it, though you were so enthusiastic and pleased with it at first. You are not meant to go off at once after every impulse that looks a good one, nor should you run away at first sight from every unwelcome sensation.

It is a good thing to apply restraint sometimes even to desires and enthusiasms that are entirely praiseworthy, otherwise your very impatience may disturb the quiet of your thoughts and your lack of discipline create a problem for the conscience of others; you may even collapse in confusion if you meet with opposition. There are even times when you must apply force and use all your strength to resist your natural desires; you must pay no attention to what human nature wants or does not want, but make it your business to see that the body is subject to the spirit, even against its will. It must be punished and made to accept its servitude, until it is ready for anything, and learns to be content with little and pleased with humble things, and not to grumble at things that do not suit it.

XII

On developing patience and resisting desires

THE DISCIPLE : O Lord God, I can see that patience is essential in this life, for there is much that goes against the grain. Whatever I do to ensure my peace, I find that fighting and suffering are inevitable.

THE LORD : That is so, my son; but I do not want you to look for the sort of peace that never feels temptation, and where obstacles are unknown. I want you to be able to feel that you have attained peace even when you are challenged by troubles, and put to the test by all kinds of opposition.

You say that you are not able to bear very much, but in that case, how will you endure the fire of purgatory? One must always choose the lesser of two evils, and so you should try to submit quietly to these present evils for God's sake, so that you may escape punishment in the future that will last for ever.

Do you imagine that worldly people have little or nothing to endure? That is not true even of those who live the softest lives. But they have a good many pleasures, you say, and do just as they please, and so they do not mind their troubles much. Even supposing they do have whatever they want, how long do you think it will last? The people that rise to greatness in this world[1] will vanish away like the smoke,[2] and there will be no remembering the delights they once enjoyed. Even while they are still alive, they are not left to enjoy their pleasures in peace, but are prey to bitterness and restlessness and fear. Often the very thing they expect to give them pleasure brings the pain of sorrow instead. They show no restraint in pursuing pleasure, and so it is only to be expected that in the end they should find shame and bitterness. These pleasures are so short-lived, so deceptive, so base, so uncontrolled, and men are so blinded and intoxicated that they cannot see it; like dumb beasts, for the little pleasure that this short life can give, they are prepared to incur the death of the soul.

My son, *do not follow the counsel of appetite. Turn thy back on thy own liking.*[3] *Have all thy longing fixed in the Lord; so he will give thee what thy heart desires.*[4]

If you really desire to experience joy and abundant comfort from me, you must scorn every earthly interest and cut off every base delight. Then you will find blessing and wealth of spiritual comfort; and as you detach yourself from the comfort of created things, you will find sweeter and more effective the comfort that comes from me.

But you will not find this comfort without a certain amount of distress and effort first. Ingrained habit will stand in your way, but a new and better habit will

[1] Ps. 72.12   [2] Ps. 36.20
[3] Ecclesiasticus 18.30   [4] Ps. 36.4

defeat it. Your natural self will rebel, but the burning
desire of the spirit will bring it under control. That old
Serpent will provoke and irritate you, but prayer will
put him to flight, and useful work block up the door
against him.

XIII

On humble submission and obedience, patterned on Jesus Christ

THE VOICE OF THE LORD : My son, anyone who tries to
escape from obedience is really escaping from grace,
and anyone who pursues private schemes loses communal blessings.

If a man does not submit to his superior gladly and
willingly, it is a sign that his old nature has not yet
learned complete obedience, but is kicking and mur-
muring still. You must learn to submit to your superior
quickly, if you desire to bring your old nature under
control. The enemy outside is defeated sooner, when
the man within is not in chaos. There is no enemy more
dangerous and troublesome to your soul than you are
to yourself when you and your spirit are not in harmony. You must learn a real indifference to self if you
want to win the victory over flesh and blood. It is
because your self-love is still undisciplined that you are
afraid to abandon yourself to the will of others.

Is there anything wonderful in the fact that you who
are dust and nothingness submit to men for God's sake,
when I, the Almighty and Most High, who created all
things from nothing, humbly submitted to men for your
sake? I became the humblest and lowest of all, so
that your pride should be broken by my humility.
Learn obedience, for you are only dust. Learn to

humble yourself and to put yourself beneath the feet of all, for you are the clay of the ground. Learn to crush your own desires, and surrender yourself in complete subjection. Savagely stamp out any sign of pride within you, and show yourself so humbled and insignificant that everyone can walk over you and tread you down like the mud of the streets.

You worthless creature, how can you complain when men find fault with you? You blackened sinner, what defence can you make? You have offended God on countless occasions, and have earned the punishment of hell. Yet your soul was precious to me, and I looked down and spared you, so that you should acknowledge my love, live in continual thankfulness for my benefits, strive towards true subjection and humility, and submit patiently when you are treated with contempt.

XIV

On reminding ourselves of the hidden judgments of God, so as to avoid over-confidence in prosperity

THE DISCIPLE: Your judgments thunder over me, Lord, and all my bones are shaken with fear and trembling. My soul is terrified. I stand appalled, and remember that *the purity of heaven itself does not suffice* you[1] The angels erred,[2] and you did not spare them.[3] What shall become of me? *The stars of heaven fell to earth.*[4] How can I exalt myself, seeing I am dust? Those who performed great deeds have fallen to the depths, and I have seen those who ate the food of angels[5] enjoying the husks of pigs.[6]

[1] Job 15.15	[2] Job 4.18
[3] II Peter 2.4	[4] Apoc. 6.13
[5] Ps. 77.25	[6] Luke 15.16

There is no holiness, Lord, if you withdraw your hand. No wisdom is of any use, if you no longer guide it. No strength can avail, if you do not preserve. No purity is safe, if you do not protect. No watchfulness on our part can effect anything unless your holy vigilance is present with us. If you abandon us, we sink and perish; but if you come to us, we are raised up and we live. We are unstable, but you make us stand firm; we are cold, but you inspire us.

How humble and meek I should feel when I look at myself! If I think I possess any good thing, how little I should value it! I must submit utterly to your fathomless judgments, O Lord, where I find that I am nothing but nothingness, utter nothingness. O immeasurable weight, impassable sea! There I can find nothing of myself but nothingness.

Where can there lurk any trace of pride, any confidence in my own goodness? All empty boasting is swallowed up in the depths of your judgments upon me. All mortal things are nothing in your sight—shall the clay bandy words with its fashioner?[7]

How can a man whose heart is really subjected to God be moved to pride and empty boasting? The whole world will not move him to pride if the Truth really has his allegiance; and he will care nothing for all the praise of men if he has built his hopes upon God. For men are all nothing, and pass away like the sound of the words they speak, but *the Lord remains faithful to his word for ever*.[8]

[7] Is. 45.9   [8] Ps. 116.2

XV

What you should feel and say when you meet something you would like

THE VOICE OF THE LORD : My son, on every such occasion this is what you should say : Lord, if this is your will, let it happen like this. Lord, if this brings you honour, let it be done in your name. Lord, if you see that this will help me and do me good, then grant that I may use it to the honour of your name. But if you know that it will harm me, and not advance my soul's salvation, then take the desire away.

The Holy Spirit is not the author of every desire that seems good and proper to you. It is not easy to decide whether it is a good spirit or an evil one that generates any particular desire, or even if it originates in your own spirit. Many find themselves deceived in the end, although they thought at first that some good spirit led them.

So whatever desirable scheme presents itself to you, you must be governed by humility and the fear of God as you work towards it; above all, you must commit it entirely to me, abandoning your own will, and saying : Lord, you know what is best. May your will decide what shall be done. Give what you will, how much you will, and when you will. Do what you know is best for me, do what pleases you and brings your name most honour. Put me where you will, and deal with me in all things as you please. I am in your hand—turn me backwards and forwards, turn me upside down. Here I am, your servant, ready for anything, for I have no desire to live for myself, but only to live perfectly and worthily for you.

A prayer that God's will may be done

Most kind Jesus, grant me your grace *to be at my side and share my labours,*[1] and remain with me right to the end. Grant that it may always be my longing and desire to do what is acceptable and pleasing to you. May your will become mine, and my will always follow yours in perfect harmony. Grant that I may be one with you in choosing and in rejecting, that I may be unable to choose or reject except as you would do.

Grant that I may die to the claims of everything in this world, and that for your sake, I may aim at being unknown and unvalued among men. Grant that beyond all my desires I may find my rest in you, and in your discover peace for my heart. You are the true peace of the heart, its only rest. All that is outside you is rough and restless. I rest in you, the highest, the everlasting Good, and *even as I lie down, sleep comes, and with sleep tranquillity.*[2]

XVI

We must expect to find true comfort in God only

THE DISCIPLE : Whatever comfort I can desire or imagine, I expect to receive not here but in the next world. Even if I had the chance of enjoying all the delights of this world, and could have all its comforts to myself, I know they could not last for long. And so, my soul, you will only find abundant comfort and complete renewal in God, who comforts the poor and champions the humble. Wait for a while, my soul. Wait for the promise of God, and you will have blessings in abundance in heaven.

If you give way to undisciplined longing for the

[1] Wisdom 9.10   [2] Ps. 4.9

things of this present life, you will lose the everlasting blessings of heaven. Make use of temporal gifts, but set your heart on eternal ones.

You cannot find complete satisfaction in any temporal gift, because you were not created to find your delight in them. Even if you possessed all the good things God has created, you could not feel happy and glad; all your gladness and happiness rest in the God who created those things. This happiness is not the sort that seems real and worth-while to the foolish people whose hearts are set on this world, but it is the happiness which the faithful followers of Christ are waiting for, and which is sometimes tasted even now by spirit-filled men with pure hearts, whose true home is in heaven.[1] The comfort offered by man is empty and short-lived; the true comfort that is rich in blessing is the gift of Truth in the heart.

The devout man has Jesus with him everywhere to be his comforter, and to him he says: Be near me, Lord Jesus, always and everywhere. Let me find my comfort in glad willingness to receive no comfort from men; and if your comfort fails me, let me accept as my highest comfort the testing that it is your righteous will to send me. For you *will not always be finding fault*; your *frown does not last for ever*.[2]

XVII

We should leave all our anxiety with God

THE VOICE OF THE LORD : My son, let me do what I want with you, since I know what is best. Your thoughts are the thoughts of a man, and you judge as your human emotions suggest.

[1] Philipp. 3.20   [2] Ps. 102.9

THE DISCIPLE : Lord, what you say is true—you care for me more than I can ever care for myself, and any man who will not leave all his care with you will stand very insecurely.

Lord, provided my will stands firm, always turned towards you, deal with me as you wish. Whatever you do with me, it can only be good. If you wish me to be in darkness, may your name be praised; if you wish me to be in the light, let me praise you again. If you graciously send me comfort, I shall praise you; if you wish me to be troubled, I shall praise you for ever just the same.

THE LORD : My son, that is the attitude you must have if you wish to walk with me. You must be just as ready to suffer as to experience joy; just as willing to be poor and empty as to be rich and full.

THE DISCIPLE : Lord, I will gladly endure for your sake whatever you wish to come my way. I am equally prepared to accept from your hand good or bad, sweet or bitter, the joyful and the sad, and for everything that happens to me, to offer you my thanks.

Keep me safe from all sin, and I will not fear death or hell. Provided you do not leave me always forsaken,[1] and do not blot me out of the book of life,[2] no misfortune that comes upon me will do me any harm.

[1] Ps. 76.8   [2] Apoc 3 5

XVIII

We must patiently endure the miseries of this life, as Christ did before us

THE VOICE OF THE LORD : My son, I came down from heaven to save you, and I accepted the miseries of your life not from necessity but from love, wanting you to learn patience and to bear the miseries of earthly life without rebelling. From the moment of my birth, right up to my death on the cross, I was never free from suffering. I knew the lack of every earthly possession, and I often heard an outcry raised against me. In compassion, I bore with humiliation and insult. For kindness I met ingratitude, for miracles, blasphemy, for teaching, criticism.

THE DISCIPLE : Lord, you lived your earthly life with patience, and in this more than anything else you obeyed your Father's command. So it is only right that a wretched sinner like me should wait in patience and obedience to your will, and for my own salvation support the burden of this life of mortality as long as you command. Even if we find this earthly life a burden, it has been made a source of merit through your grace; and your example and the traces left by the saints who followed you have made it brighter and easier for weaker people to bear. Besides, there is more comfort now than there was under the Old Law, when the door of heaven remained firmly shut and even the road to heaven seemed darker, when there were so few who cared to look for the heavenly kingdom. Indeed, until your passion and sacred death, there was no way into the heavenly kingdom, even for those who were righteous and destined to be saved.

What endless thanks I owe you for graciously showing me and all who believe in you the straight good road to your eternal kingdom. For the life you lived is our life, and by holy patience we travel towards you, our reward at the end of the journey. If you had not gone before and told us what to do, would anyone try to follow? It is a sad thought that many people would not get very far if they could not fix their eyes on your shining example. Our enthusiasm is so lukewarm even when we have been told what you did and taught. What would happen if we did not have so bright a light to guide us as we follow?

XIX

How injury should be accepted, and how real patience is revealed

THE VOICE OF THE LORD : What is that I hear you saying, my son? Look at my sufferings and the sufferings of the saints, and stop complaining. *Your battle against sin has not yet called for bloodshed.*[1] What you have to face is hardly anything compared with the real sufferings of those who have met strong temptations and been hard pressed and tested and tried out time and time again. Turn over in your mind the heavy trials of others, and your own insignificant ones will be easier to bear. If you do not think they are insignificant, take care that it is not your lack of patience that causes that as well.

But whether they are great or small, aim at bearing

[1] Hebr. 12.4

them all with patience. If you make up your mind to submit to these things patiently, you will be acting wisely and will acquire more merit. Besides, you will find them easier to bear, if you work hard to develop the right attitude and make it into a habit.

You must not say, ' I am quite unable to submit to this sort of thing, coming from a man like that; and it is not the sort of thing I should be asked to accept—he has done me a great deal of harm, and accused me of something that never entered my head. Still, I would accept it from another man, provided I thought it the sort of thing I should be asked to accept.'

This kind of thinking is very foolish. It is always weighing up what injuries it has received from which people, instead of keeping it in mind that there is a virtue in patience, and that a reward awaits it from God. A man is not really patient if he is only prepared to submit to what he thinks right from the person whom he chooses. The really patient man does not mind who it is that puts him to the test—whether it is his superior, or an equal, or a subordinate; whether it is a good, holy man, or a wicked and unworthy one. Whenever anything happens that is hard to bear, however difficult it is and whoever causes it, he accepts it all with thanks as a gift from the hand of God. In his eyes it is a great benefit, because God will not let anything that is endured for his sake, however small it is, pass by without reward.

So if you want to be victorious, you must be ready for a fight. The only way to win a crown for endurance is to take part in a struggle. You reject any chance of the crown if you refuse to endure; but if you want the crown, you must boldly engage in the struggle and face all that comes with patience. The road to rest must pass through toil, and there is no victory that is not preceded by a battle.

THE DISCIPLE : Lord, I see I cannot do this by nature—

make me able to do it by grace. You know that I am
not able to endure very much, and that I am downcast
by the slightest difficulty. Grant that for your sake I
may come to love and desire any hardship that puts me
to the test, for salvation is brought to my soul when I
undergo suffering and trouble for you.

XX

*A confession of weakness, and a consideration of
the miseries of this life*

THE DISCIPLE : *Fault of mine, said I, I here confess to
the Lord.*[1]

I will confess my weakness to you, Lord. Often it is
such a small thing that makes me downcast and sad. I
make up my mind to act boldly, and when a little
temptation comes, I suffer anguish out of all proportion.
Sometimes it is quite an unimportant thing that gives
rise to serious temptation; and just when I think I am
safe for a while, before I realize what is happening, a
little gust of wind almost has me over.

O Lord, I come abjectly before you; see this weakness which you already know so well. Take pity on me,
save me from sinking in the mire,[2] do not leave me
lying dejected for ever. I am struck down and filled
with shame in your presence by the thought that I fall
so easily and have no strength to resist my desires.
Even if I do not give way to them, they still attack
continually, and I find it worrying and hard; one grows
so tired of living in continual strife like this. And
what makes me so aware of my weakness is that these
abominable imaginings never go away as quickly as
they come.

[1] Ps. 31.5   [2] Ps. 68.15

Great God of Israel, lover of faithful souls—take pity on the labours and sorrows of your servant, and be at his side wherever he goes.[3] Make me strong with the strength of heaven, or else the old self, my hateful flesh, will lord it over me; for my spirit as yet cannot control my flesh, and as long as this life of sorrows is mine, I must battle against it.

What a life this is! There is no end to trouble and sorrow, and everything is full of snares and enemies. When one trial or temptation goes away, another comes, and sometimes we are still wrestling with the previous problem when new ones are suddenly added to it.

How can we love life when it brings so much bitterness and is exposed to so many misfortunes and so much unhappiness? How can we even call it life, when it brings so much death and destruction? Yet we do love it, and many people expect to find happiness in it. We often blame this world for its deceitfulness and unreality, and yet we find it hard to renounce it because the corrupt desires of the body still have too much power. Some things make us love the world, while others turn us against it. What makes us love the world is the *gratification of corrupt nature, gratification of the eye, the empty pomp of living*;[4] but these things bring their own punishment with all its misery, and then we begin to feel hatred and loathing of the world. But the sad thing is that base pleasures still win the day in the worldly mind, and it imagines that the thorns are concealing something sweet. This is because it has never caught a glimpse or had a taste of the sweetness of God, or the inward joy of goodness.

But to those who reject the world completely and submit to the holy discipline of the cloister in order to live for God, that divine delight, promised to those who truly leave all, is surely given; and so they see how often the world is led astray and how mistaken it is.

[3] Jos. 1.9   [4] John 2.16

XXI

Above all God's gifts, our ultimate rest is in him

THE DISCIPLE: My soul, in everything and yet beyond everything, you must find your rest in the Lord, for he is the eternal rest of the saints.

Most sweet and beloved Jesus, grant that I may find my rest in you beyond all that you have created; beyond all health and beauty, all glory and honour; beyond power and rank, knowledge and ability; beyond riches and talents; beyond gladness and joy; beyond fame and reputation; beyond sweetness and comfort; beyond hopes and promises, rewards and desires; beyond all the gifts and favours that are in your power to give, beyond all the gladness and rejoicing that are in our power to feel; beyond angels and archangels, and all the host of heaven, beyond all things visible and invisible, beyond anything which is not you, O God.

My Lord and my God, you are good above all that is good. You alone are most high, most mighty, most sufficient, most complete; you alone are full of sweetness, of comfort, of beauty and love; you alone are exalted and glorious above all things; and in you all good things have their perfect existence, as they always have done and as they always shall. Therefore I am not satisfied by anything you give me that is not yourself, nor by any promise or revelation that does not let me see you and receive you fully. My heart cannot really rest or find full satisfaction unless it rests in you,[1] soaring beyond all your gifts, beyond the whole creation.

O Jesus Christ, bridegroom beloved, lover most pure, ruler of all creation, who will give me the wings of true liberty, so that I may fly away to rest in you?

[1] Augustine, *Confessions* 1.1

When shall I know freedom from all things, when shall I really see how gracious, O Lord my God, you are?[2] When shall I be able to still every thought and gaze on you?—then shall I forget myself in love of you, and leaving the common ways of prayer, pass beyond all sense and measure, and be conscious only of you.

But as it is, I often cry out in grief; I groan beneath the load of my unhappy state. This vale of sorrows is full of countless evils which worry and sadden me, and fill my life with gloom; they hinder me and distract me, entice and ensnare me, and so I cannot approach you without hindrance, and enjoy that sweet embrace of yours which the blessed spirits know continually.

O Jesus, radiance of the eternal splendour,[3] and comfort of the pilgrim soul, pity my sighs, and the utter desolation I suffer here on earth. Even when I do not speak, my face is before you, and my silence cries out to you. How long will my Lord put off his coming? If only he would come to his poor servant and make him glad. If only he would stretch out his hand and snatch his wretched follower out of all his misery. O come, O come, for no day or hour will know happiness without you. You are my joy, and without you my table is bare. I am a pitiful wretch, a prisoner lying in chains, until you cheer me with the light of your presence and give me my freedom, and look on me with love. Others may fill their lives with many things in place of you, but nothing will ever content me, O God, until I have you, my hope and eternal salvation. I will not hold my tongue or cease to pray to you, until your grace returns and you speak to me in my heart.

THE LORD : See, I am here, I have come because you called me. Your tears and the longing of your soul, the repentance and humbling of your heart moved me and brought me to you.

[2] Ps. 33.9   [3] Hebr. 1.3

THE DISCIPLE: Lord, I called out to you because I longed for you; I was prepared to give up everything else if I could only have you. Yet it was you that first moved me and made me look for you. Blessings on your name, O Lord, for you have shown your servant this goodness out of the richness of your mercy. What can your servant say as he stands before you? He can only humble himself before you, remembering his sinfulness and worthlessness. In all the wonders of heaven and earth there is nothing that approaches you; your works are very good, your judgments true, and all things are guided by your providence. O Wisdom of the Father, may praise and glory be yours; my lips shall bring you praise and blessings, my soul shall praise you with the whole creation.

XXII

On considering God's many different gifts

THE DISCIPLE: O Lord, teach my heart to understand your laws and show me how to walk in obedience to your commands. Make me know what is your will for me, and help me to consider all your good gifts, both in general and in particular, with such reverence and careful thought that, from now on, I may offer you thanks as I should. Yet I know and confess that I cannot offer you the thankful praise I owe for even the smallest thing. I am less than all the good things I have received, and when I consider your generosity, my spirit falters and I cannot take it in.

All our powers of body and spirit, every gift both natural and supernatural, outward or inward, comes as a blessing from you, and reveals your goodness, generosity and love, for you have given us all that is good.

One man may receive more, and another less; but all

the gifts are yours, and without you no man can possess anything at all.

If a man receives more, he has no right to boast of his merits, or think himself superior to other men, or treat with contempt those who have less than himself; it is the man who takes the least credit to himself, and shows the greatest humility and devotion in offering thanks to God, who is really the greatest and best. It is the man who has the humblest opinion of himself and thinks himself quite unworthy of receiving any gift who is the most fitted to receive great gifts.

If a man receives less, he must not feel miserable or aggrieved about it, or envy the man with more, but he should turn his eyes on you and praise your goodness, because you pour out your gifts so richly, so generously and so freely, making no distinction between man and man.[1] All gifts come from you, and it is you we must praise for them all.

You know what is best to give each one; and since it is clear to you what each man's merits are, it is for you and not for us to decide why one has less and another more.

And so, O Lord God, I can even consider it a great blessing if I do not have much to bring me praise and glory from men; for when a man does not have much, he can look at his poverty and worthlessness, and far from feeling burdened and sorrowful and dejected, he can feel comforted and glad, for it is the poor and humble and despised in the eyes of the world that you have chosen, O God, to be the familiar members of your household.

Your apostles bear witness to this, for you have divided *a world between them for their domains*.[2] Yet they spent their lives in this world without complaint, and were so humble and devoid of pride, so completely free of all malice and guile, that they rejoiced to suffer

---

[1] Acts 10.34; Gal. 2.6   [2] Ps. 44.17

humiliation for your sake, and gladly embraced things that the world regards with horror.

If a man loves you and acknowledges your goodness, he should find joy above all else in the fulfilment in his own life of your will and of your everlasting decree. That should bring him so much contentment and happiness that he is just as ready to be the least as others are to be greatest; just as peaceful and contented in the lowest place as he would be in the highest, and just as ready to be despised and rejected and have no fame or reputation, as to be honoured and important. Your will and the love of your honour should mean more than all other things, and bring more comfort and happiness than all the blessings he has received or expects to receive.

XXIII

Four things that bring great peace

THE VOICE OF THE LORD : My son, I will teach you the way of peace and true liberty.

THE DISCIPLE : Do this, O Lord—I am eager to hear.

THE LORD : My son, try to do another's will rather than your own. Always choose to have less rather than more. Always choose the lowest place and to be less than everyone else. Always long and pray that the will of God may be fully realized in your life. You will find that the man who does all this walks in the land of peace and quietness.

THE DISCIPLE : Lord, what you say is brief, but there is much perfection in it. It is short in words, but rich in wisdom and abounding in fruit. If only I could observe it faithfully, I would not be so easily disturbed. Whenever I feel weighed down and see that my peace is gone, I find that I have drifted from this teaching.

You can do all things, and you always love to see the soul making progress—increase the gift of grace, so that I can do what you say, and work out my salvation.

A prayer against evil thoughts

O God, do not keep thy distance from me; hasten my God to aid me.[1] Great fears and imaginings of all kinds have combined to attack my soul. How can I come through them unharmed? How can I crush them?

I will still lead thee on thy way, says the Lord, *bending the pride of earth low before thee.* I will open the doors of the prison, and *hidden treasures I will hand over to thee.*[2]

O Lord, do as you say, and may all my evil imaginings flee from your presence. My only hope and comfort is to take refuge with you in all my troubles, to trust you, to call out to you from my inmost heart, and patiently wait till you send your comfort.

A prayer for enlightenment of mind

Good Jesus, enlighten me with the brightness of the inward light, and from the hiding places of my heart bring out all that is dark. Curb the many wanderings of my thoughts, and crush the temptations that press me so hard. Fight powerfully for me, drive from their strongholds the evil desires that lurk to entrap me; then there will be *peace within thy ramparts,*[3] and abundant praise will re-echo in the sacred temple that my purified heart shall become. Check the wind and the storms; say to the sea 'Be still,' and 'Do not blow' to the wind; then there will be deep calm.[4]

[1] Ps. 70.12   [2] Is. 45.2-3   [3] Ps. 121.7   [4] Matt. 8.26

The light of thy presence, the fulfilment of thy promise, let these be my escort.[5]

Shed your light on the earth, for until you enlighten me, I am earth that is empty and waste.[6] Shed your grace on me from above; bathe my heart in the dew of heaven, and bring in the waters of devotion, so that the face of the earth may be watered, and good fruit be produced, fruit that is the best. Lift up this soul of mine that is crushed with the weight of sins; draw all my desire up to the things of heaven, so that when I have once tasted the joys of the world above, I may find no pleasure in the thought of earthly things.

Carry me away, part me from the transient comfort of created things, for nothing that is created can assuage and satisfy my longing. Join me to yourself in the unbreakable bond of love, for you alone can satisfy the yearning of my love, and all things are meaningless without you.

XXIV

On avoiding inquisitive interest in another's life

THE VOICE OF THE LORD : My son, you must not be inquisitive and burden yourself with useless cares. All that is no concern of yours—*do thou follow me.*[1] It does not matter to you whether that man is good or bad, or what this man does and says—you will not be asked to answer for other people, but you will have to account for yourself. So why involve yourself in other people's lives? I know all men, I see everything that happens under the sun; I know the state of every man; I know what he thinks, what he desires, and what his intentions really aim at. So you should entrust it all to me, and preserve yourself in quietness and peace, leav-

[5] Ps. 42.3   [6] Gen. 1.2   [1] John 21.22

ing the other man to create what disturbance he pleases. Whatever he does or says will be on his own head, because he cannot deceive me.

You must not be interested in acquiring ' the shadow of a mighty name,'[2] or gathering a wide circle of acquaintance, or winning personal affection. All these things are the source of distraction and of darkness in the heart. I would gladly speak to you and show you my secrets, if only you would watch eagerly for my coming, and open the door of your heart. Live carefully, *keep your senses awake to greet the hours of prayer,*[3] and show yourself humble in all things.

XXV

The basis of unshakeable peace and real progress

THE VOICE OF THE LORD : My son, this is what I once said : *Peace is my bequest to you, and the peace which I will give you is mine to give; I do not give peace as the world gives it.*[1]

Everyone desires peace, but not everyone cares for the things that bring real peace. My peace is given to those who are humble and gentle in their hearts, and your peace will lie in being very patient. If you listen to me and do what I tell you, you will enjoy great peace.
THE DISCIPLE : What do you want me to do?
THE LORD : At all times keep your attention fixed on what you are doing and saying, and let your whole aim be to please me and me alone, not seeking or desiring anything outside me. As for the words and actions of

    [2] Lucan, *Pharsalia* i. 135; *v.* St Bernard, *Sermons (I in circum. Domini,* Migne 183, col. 133)
    [3] I Peter 4.7   [1] John 14.27

others, keep yourself from making rash judgments, and do not concern yourself with things that are not your business. Then perhaps you will be free from serious disturbance—but you cannot expect to escape all disturbance during this earthly life, and to be free from all distress of mind and body. That belongs to the peace and quiet of eternity.

So you must not imagine that you have found true peace if you are not conscious of any burden; nor must you think all is well if no one stands in your way; you have not achieved perfection just because everything seems to be going the way you would like it. And if you find yourself in a state of great devotion and happiness, you must not begin to have high ideas and imagine that God loves you more than others. It is not these things that pick out the true lover of goodness, and indicate progress and growth in perfection.

THE DISCIPLE: Then what does show these things, Lord?

THE LORD: They are shown by the wholehearted surrender of yourself to the will of God, so that you no longer want your own way in anything, great or small, in time or in eternity, but go on thanking God cheerfully amidst prosperity and adversity, laying no more weight on one than on the other. If you have enough courage, patience and trust, when the inward comfort is taken from you, to prepare yourself for even harder things, and instead of complaining that you have done nothing to deserve such suffering, to accept my justice and praise my holiness whatever I send you, then you will be walking the paths of real peace, and will feel assured of seeing my face and experiencing joy again. For if you achieve complete disregard of self, you will enjoy abundant peace, as far as living in this world allows you to do so.

XXVI

The pre-eminence of a free mind, which is produced by humble prayer, not study

THE DISCIPLE : O Lord, it is the perfect man who can keep his mind intent on heavenly things, and pass through all the cares of this life without a sign of care —not because he is insensitive, but enjoying the prerogative of a free mind which clings to no created thing with undisciplined affection.

Most merciful God, keep me, I pray, from being engrossed by the cares of this life; keep me from falling victim to pleasure through my body's needs; keep me from defeat and despair when my soul is molested and hindered.

I do not ask you to save me from the things which this foolish world desires so ardently, but from the miseries due to the common curse of mankind, which drag down the soul of your servant and hold him back so that he cannot enter into the liberty of the spirit whenever he would like.

O God, sweetness ineffable, make bitter for me all earthly comfort that draws me away from love of eternal things and entices me towards itself with the sight of present pleasure. Save me, O my God, save me from defeat by flesh and blood; do not let the world and its brief glory lead me astray; do not let the Devil and his cunning overthrow me. Give me boldness in resisting, patience in enduring, firmness in persevering. In place of all the joys of the world grant the sweet anointing of your spirit, and instead of the loves of this life, pour in the love of your name.

See what a burden is laid on the burning spirit by the need for food and drink and clothing and all the other things which keep the body alive. Grant that I may not become too fond of these things for their own sake, but may use them all with moderation. I cannot give them up altogether since the body needs some care, but the holy law forbids me to seek more than I need, merely to give myself pleasure. Otherwise the body will rebel against the spirit. I pray that amid all these things your hand may guide and teach me, and keep me from excess in anything.

XXVII

Love of self holds you back from the highest good

THE VOICE OF THE LORD : My son, to receive everything you must give everything, and not own yourself at all. Realize that love of self does you more harm than anything the world can produce. It is only because you have an inclination for them that things prove hard to shake off; if your love were pure, simple and properly controlled, you would find yourself set free from the bondage of things.

Do not desire things which you are not allowed to possess; do not possess things which may prove a hindrance and rob you of your inward freedom.

It is strange that you do not entrust yourself to me from the depths of your heart, with all the things you may ever possess or want to possess. Why let yourself be eaten up with useless worries, worn out with pointless cares? Accept what is my will for you, and you will suffer no loss.

You will never be happy or content if you hope to acquire something or go somewhere, in order to advance your own interests and get your own way. In everything there will be something to disappoint you, and wherever you go, someone will stand in your way.

You will not find happiness in multiplying external possessions, but in despising them and rooting them out of the heart. This applies not only to wealth and riches, but to ambition for honours and desire for empty praise, which all pass away with the world.

You will find little help from the place you are in, if the spirit of fervour is missing; and a peace that depends on outward things will not last long, if your heart is away from its true foundation. If you do not rest in me, you may change your state but not improve it; when the right time comes, you will find the very thing you tried to escape, and something more besides.

A prayer for purity of heart and heavenly wisdom

O God, make me strong with the grace of the Holy Spirit; strengthen me with a power that reaches my innermost being,[1] so that I may empty my heart of all useless cares and worries, and no longer be torn with desire for anything, whatever it may be worth, but may know that all things pass away, and that I am passing with them. For the sun shines on nothing that is lasting, but everything here is unreal and an affliction to the spirit. How wise a man is if he knows it!

O Lord, grant me heavenly wisdom, so that I may learn above all things to seek you and to find you, above all things to delight in you and love you; and to value everything else according to its place in your wise plan.

Grant me the sense to turn a deaf ear to flattery, and patience to bear with contradiction; for it is true wisdom to stand unmoved amidst the changing breeze

[1] Eph. 3.16

of men's words, and to give no heed to the seductive voice of the siren. So we shall go on in safety on the road we have begun.

XXVIII

Against maligning tongues

THE VOICE OF THE LORD : My son, you must not take it badly if some people have a low opinion of you, and say things that are not very pleasant to hear. You should have an even lower opinion of yourself, and consider that you are more likely to err than anyone.

If you are treading the path of the inward life, you will not give much thought to words that soon fly past. It is no small wisdom to keep silent when times are difficult, and to turn to me in your heart, not letting men's judgments disturb you.

You must not let your peace depend on what men say. Whether they judge you favourably or adversely, that does not make you any different from what you are.

True peace and true glory can only be found in me, and the secret of great peace is to have no desire to please men, and no fear of displeasing them either. It is your undisciplined affections and your foolish fears that make your senses restless and destroy the peace of your heart.

XXIX

In the midst of troubles, we must call on God and bless him

THE DISCIPLE : May your name, O Lord, be blessed for
ever, for it is your will that this testing and time of
trouble should come upon me. I cannot flee from it,
but must flee to you for refuge, so that you can help
me and turn it to a blessing.

O Lord, the difficult time is upon me now and I
am not at peace in my heart, but this present suffering
is proving very hard to bear. Beloved Father, what
shall I say? Troubles hem me in on every side. *Save
me from undergoing this hour of trial—and yet I have
only reached this hour of trial that I might undergo
it,*[1] and bring glory to your name; for it is you that
shall deliver me when I have been brought low. O
Lord, be willing to rescue me, for I am helpless; what
can I do, where can I go without you? Grant me
patience, Lord, on this occasion too. Help me, O my
God, and I shall not be afraid, however heavy my
burden.

And now in the midst of all my trouble, this is what I
shall say : O Lord, your will be done, for I deserve
burdens and troubles—in any case, I must submit to it,
until the storm goes by and things are better. O help me
do so with patience! Yet your almighty hand can take
away even this temptation, and shield me from it, so
that I do not give way completely under its blows. O
God of mercy, you have done this so often for me; and
the harder it seems to me, the easier it is for the Most
High to *alter the fashion of his dealings with men.*[2]

[1] John 12.27   [2] Ps. 76.11

XXX

On asking for God's help, and believing that you will regain the state of grace

THE VOICE OF THE LORD : My son, I am the Lord, no strength like mine in the hour of distress.[1] Come to me, when things are hard for you.

The greatest obstacle to heavenly comfort is your slowness in turning to prayer. Before you start praying to me in earnest, you look for comforts of every kind, and try to find relief for your soul in external things. And so you find little help in any of them. In the end, you have to realize that I am the one that saves men when they put their trust in me, and that outside me there is no effective aid, no reliable counsel, no lasting remedy.

But when your spirit revives after the storm, you shall grow strong again beneath the clear sky of my mercies. I am near, says the Lord, to restore all things, not merely to their former state, but adding heaped-up, overflowing riches. Is any task too difficult for me? Shall I be like a man who promises and does not keep his word? Where is your faith? Take a firm stand, and persevere. Show patience and courage—comfort will come to you in due time. Wait for me, wait—I will come and heal you.[2]

This alarm you feel is nothing but a temptation; the fears that worry you are groundless. What is the good of worrying about things that may be going to happen? That only adds one misery to another. *For today, today's troubles are enough.*[3] There is not much point either in fearing the future or in looking forward to it,

[1] Nahum 1.7   [2] Matt. 8.7   [3] Matt. 6.34

when the things you imagine may well never come to pass. It is human nature to be deluded by this sort of thinking; and it is clear that the spirit is still weak when it accepts the Enemy's suggestions with so little resistance. He does not mind whether he uses reality or fantasy, so long as he tricks men and gives them false ideas; it is all the same to him whether it is attachment to the present or fear of the future that lets him trip them up. *So do not let your heart be distressed, or play the coward. Have faith in me.*[4] Have confidence in my mercy. When you think you are a long way from me, I am often quite near; when you imagine that everything is lost, you are often on the point of acquiring great merit. Everything is not lost just because something goes wrong. You must never judge by what you happen to be feeling; and whenever life is proving difficult for any reason whatsoever, you must not abandon hope and behave as if things would never improve. Do not imagine you have been utterly abandoned, even if I send you distress for a time, or take away some comfort. That is what the journey to the heavenly kingdom involves.

For you, as for my other servants, it is definitely much better to be exercised by adversity than to have everything to your satisfaction. I know your secret thoughts; I know that your salvation is furthered if you are left from time to time with life that seems tasteless; otherwise you might become arrogant in prosperity, and feel self-satisfied over something that is not due to yourself. What I have given, I can take away, and I can give it back again when it pleases me. When I have given it, it is still mine; when I take it back, I am not removing anything of yours. *Whatever gifts are worth having, whatever endowments are perfect of their kind,*[5] they are all mine. If I send you some burden, something that goes against the grain, you must not feel ill-used

---

[4] John 14.27, 14.1   [5] James 1.17

or down-hearted—I can soon take it away, and turn
the heaviness of your heart to joy. And when I treat
you like this, I am still righteous and worthy of praise.

If you are really wise and can see things as they
really are, you should never be saddened or disheart-
ened when things are difficult. You should rejoice and
give thanks instead. Indeed, you should think it your
chief joy if I will but torment you to your death.[6] *I
have bestowed my love upon you, just as my Father
has bestowed his love upon me*[7]—that is what I said to
my beloved disciples, and I did not send them out to
experience joy in this life, but to endure great struggles;
I sent them not to be honoured but to be despised, not
to idleness but to toil, not to rest, but to *endure and
yield a harvest*.[8] My son, remember these words of
mine.

XXXI

*On neglecting the whole creation in order to find
the Creator*

THE DISCIPLE : O Lord, I need far more grace than I
have now, if I am ever to reach a state in which neither
man nor any other creature can be a hindrance to me.
As long as there is anything to hold me back, I cannot
freely fly up to you. I long to be free and fly to you,
like the man who cried, *Had I but wings as a dove has
wings, to fly away and find rest!*[1]

There is nothing more at rest than the eye that can
gaze without distraction, nothing more free than the
man who desires nothing on this earth. So we must
pass beyond the whole creation, and lose all consciousness of self; then stand in ecstasy and see that you, the

[6] Job 6.10   [7] John 15.9   [8] Luke 8.15   [1] Ps. 54.7

creator of all things, have nothing that approaches you among the whole creation.

Only if a man is loosed from all created things is he free to direct his will to the things of God. The reason why so few contemplatives are found is that few people know how to cut themselves off completely from all that is perishable and created. To do so one needs a great grace that can raise the soul and transport it beyond itself.

Unless a man is uplifted in spirit, released from the ties of every created thing and wholly united to God, it does not matter much what he knows or possesses. He will long remain spiritually weak and unable to rise, if he thinks anything of value other than the one immeasurable, eternal Good. Whatever is not God is nothing, and must be considered nothing.

There is a great difference between the wisdom of a devout, spiritually enlightened man, and the knowledge of a learned and studious scholar. The teaching which the divine influence pours into our souls from above is far more noble than the learning which man acquires by so much mental effort.

There are many who desire contemplation, but they are not eager to practise what it demands. They are much hindered because they depend on things which can be seen and perceived with the senses, and because they have hardly started to put the old nature to death. I do not know why it is, or by what spirit we are led, or what we so-called spiritual men are after, that we expend much labour and more care on worthless and impermanent things, and hardly ever still our restless senses and give our attention fully to what lies within. We concentrate for a brief time, and then unfortunately our thoughts break away again; we do not subject our actions to a really searching scrutiny; we fail to notice the low level of our affections; and we do not regret the impurity of everything we do.

There was *no creature on earth but had lost its true direction*,[2] and that was why the great Flood came. Since the desires of our hearts have gone astray, it is inevitable that our actions should reveal our lack of inner strength and also miss the way. It is from a pure heart that the harvest of a good life comes.

Men ask what a man has done, but they are not so meticulous in considering what motivates his actions. They ask if he has been strong, rich, handsome, clever, a good writer, a good singer, or a good workman; but often nothing is said of his lowliness in spirit, his patience, his gentleness, his devotion to God, the quality of his inner life. It is man's natural instinct to consider outward characteristics, grace looks at those within. So man is often mistaken, but grace rests its hope on God, and so is not deceived.

XXXII

On denying one's own claims and renouncing every desire

THE VOICE OF THE LORD: My son, you cannot have complete freedom unless you deny your own claims entirely. Men are in chains as long as they have possessions and love their own interests, as long as they are covetous, curious and unsettled, always looking for what is easy and not for the way of Jesus Christ, fashioning and building something that will not last. For everything will perish that does not spring from God.

Hold on to the brief saying that sums this up—Leave everything and you will find everything; abandon desire and you will discover rest. Meditate on it, and

[2] Gen. 6.12

when you have put it into practice, you will understand everything.

THE DISCIPLE : O Lord, that is not child's play, nor the work of a single day. These few words contain the full perfection of the religious.

THE LORD : My son, you must not be discouraged or take fright when you hear of the way of those who have been made perfect. You should rather be spurred on to reach the heights, or at least to aspire earnestly towards them. If only you had reached the state in which you no longer loved yourself, but stood wholly ready to do my will and the will of the father I have set over you. Then you would please me very much, and your whole life would pass in joy and peace. As it is, there are still many things that you must give up, and unless you resign them entirely to me, you will not achieve the thing for which you pray.

My counsel to thee is to come and buy from me what thou needest; gold proved in the fire, to make thee rich.[1] And that gold is the heavenly wisdom that tramples underfoot all that is base. Set this above earthly wisdom, all that brings you a reputation and makes you pleased with yourself.

It is a poor thing I have told you to buy when compared with the treasures of earth. The true heavenly wisdom has no high opinion of itself and does not seek earthly glory, and so it seems a poor and worthless object, almost forgotten by men. Many of them preach it with their mouths, but their lives show little sign of it. Yet it is that pearl of great cost,[2] that only a few can find.

[1] Apoc. 3.18   [2] Matt. 13.46

XXXIII

On the fickleness of the heart, and on keeping one's ultimate intention fixed on God

THE VOICE OF THE LORD : My son, you must not rely on how you feel at the moment, for you will soon feel something quite different. As long as you remain in this life, you cannot help being subject to change—sometimes you are happy, sometimes sad; sometimes peaceful, sometimes troubled; sometimes devout, sometimes quite unmoved; sometimes full of enthusiasm, sometimes full of apathy; sometimes serious, sometimes taking nothing seriously at all.

Yet the man who is wise and spiritually educated stands above these shifting emotions; he pays no attention to his personal feelings; he does not care from what quarter the wind of his fickleness is blowing, but sees to it that the whole purpose of his mind is striving towards its proper longed-for goal. A man can remain unshaken, one and the same, if across all the different things that intervene, he directs his will with undivided gaze and without a moment's slackening to me.

The purer the eye of the will, the more unswerving the course amidst the squalls. But the clear eye of the will is dimmed in many people, because they are so ready to look away at any pleasant thing that comes across their path—it is rare to find a man who is wholly free from the blemish of self-seeking. That was why the Jews once came to Martha and Mary at Bethany, *not only on account of Jesus, but so as to have sight of Lazarus.*[1]

[1] John 12.9

So you must clear the eye of your will, so that its gaze is undivided and direct, and turn it towards me past all the various things that lie between.

XXXIV

One who loves God finds him satisfying above all things and in all things

THE DISCIPLE: Behold my God and my all. What more can I want? What more blessed thing can I desire? How full of sweetness and delight these words seem to a man who loves the Word, and not the world and what the world has to offer.[1]

My God and my all! No other words are needed if a man understands; and if he loves, there is joy in repeating them often. For when you are with us all things give delight; when you are not there, everything is tasteless. You give the tranquil heart, great peace, and festal gladness. It is you that make us feel content with everything, able to praise you in everything; and without you nothing can please us for long. If anything is to please us and taste good to our souls, it must contain your grace and be seasoned with your wisdom. The man who finds you sweet will find the right savour in all things, but nothing can give pleasure to the man who finds no sweetness in you.

Those who have a taste for worldly wisdom and all that is valued by the natural man have no knowledge of your wisdom; for the world is full of folly and the desires of the natural man mean death. But when a man disregards earthly things, puts the old nature to death and follows you, it is clear that he has a taste for

[1] I John 2.15

the real wisdom. He is reorientated from deception to truth, from corrupt nature to the spirit. It is God who tastes good to him, and whatever good thing he meets in the creation, he turns it all to the praise of his Creator. Different, very different indeed, is the savour of the Creator and the creature, of eternity and time, of light uncreated and light made visible.

O eternal light, surpassing all created lights, brandish your lightnings[2] from the heights and pierce my inmost heart. Purify my spirit with all its powers; bring gladness, light and life, so that I may hold fast to you in joyful ecstasy. O when will that blessed time come, that time I long for, when your presence satisfies me wholly, and you are to me all in all? Until that gift is given, joy cannot be complete.

But to my sorrow, the old nature still lives on within me; it is not yet crucified, it is not yet entirely dead. It is still at war with the impulses of the spirit,[3] it still stirs up strife within me, and will not leave the kingdom of my soul in peace.

It is thou that dost curb the pride of the sea and calm the tumult of its waves.[4] O rise up and help me. *Scatter the nations that delight in war;*[5] crush them in your might; show, I pray, your mighty works, and let your right hand bring you glory; for I have no hope or refuge except in you, my Lord, my God.

---

[2] Ps. 143.6   [3] Gal. 5.17   [4] Ps. 88.10   [5] Ps. 67.31

XXXV

There is no security from temptation in this life

THE VOICE OF THE LORD : My son, you are never safe in this life, but at every moment as long as you are alive you need your spiritual weapons. You are moving among enemies who attack on the right and the left. If you do not use your shield of patience at every point, it will not be long before you are wounded. In addition, if you do not fix your heart unshakeably on me, with the solid intention of bearing everything for my sake, you will not be able to endure the heat of battle, or attain the prize of the blessed. You must press on boldly through every experience, and deal forcibly with all that stands in your way. For it is to the victorious that *the hidden manna* is given,[1] while the man who does not stir himself is left with misery.

If you are looking for rest in this life, how will you ever reach the everlasting rest at the end? It is not rest you must expect, but suffering. Look for your true peace not on earth, but in heaven, not in men or in other creatures, but in God alone. For love of God you should be prepared to endure anything—toil, pain, temptation, vexation, anxiety, need, weakness, injustice, slander, blame, humiliation, shame, censure and contempt. Such things strengthen virtue; they test the soldier of Christ and make up his heavenly crown. In return for your brief labours I will give you an eternal reward; for your passing humiliation, glory that will never end.

Do you imagine that spiritual comfort can be yours

[1] Apoc. 2.17

all the time for the asking? Not even my saints had that experience, but they suffered many hardships, all kinds of temptations, and times of utter desolation. But in every experience they held on in patience, trusting in God rather than themselves, knowing that these present sufferings are not to be counted as the measure of that glory,[2] nor sufficient to win it. Do you want to have at once what other people have passed through much sorrow and toil to achieve? Wait for the Lord, act like a man, be strong; do not lose faith and do not run away, but resolutely expose to danger both mind and body for the glory of God. I will reward you most abundantly, and I will be with you in all that is difficult.

XXXVI

Men's censure is unimportant

THE VOICE OF THE LORD : My son, let your heart rest firmly in the Lord, and have no fear of men's condemnation while your conscience assures you that you are innocent and right with God. It is a good and blessed thing to suffer like this, and it will not prove hard for the humble heart that trusts God rather than itself.

People are many and they say a great deal, and that is why one should give them little credit. Besides, it is impossible to satisfy everyone. Paul's desire was to please everyone in the Lord, and he was everything by turns to everybody,[1] yet he made little account of men's scrutiny or of any human audit-day.[2] He did everything in his power for the salvation and spiritual growth of others, but he could not always avoid their censure and contempt. For that reason, he committed the whole affair to God, who understood it wholly, and

[2] Rom. 8.18   [1] I Cor. 9.22   [2] I Cor. 4.3

defended himself by patience and humility against those who spoke ill of him or invented lying tales and spread them about. Still, he did give them an answer sometimes, so that he should not hurt the conscience of weaker Christians by his unwillingness to speak.

And is it thou that art afraid of mortal man?[3]—he is here today and gone tomorrow. Fear God, and you will have no terror of men. How can any man harm you by evil word or deed? He hurts himself rather than you, and whoever he is, he cannot escape God's judgment. Keep God before your eyes, and do not argue or try to justify yourself. If for the moment your opponent seems to get the better of you, and you suffer undeserved humiliation, do not feel aggrieved or let impatience take some brightness from your crown. Instead look up to me in heaven, for I am able to deliver from all hurt and humiliation, and to *award to every man what his acts have deserved.*[4]

XXXVII

On surrendering oneself wholly and entirely in order to know liberty of spirit

THE VOICE OF THE LORD : My son, give up self and you will find me. Lose the right to choose and the right to own, and you will know nothing but gain. Abundant grace will be heaped upon you the moment you surrender your own will and do not claim it back again.

THE DISCIPLE : O Lord, when shall I surrender myself? at what point give up my claims?

THE LORD : Always and at every moment, in small

[3] Is. 51.12   [4] Rom. 2.6

things and in great. I allow no exceptions, but want to find you naked of everything. Besides, how can you be mine or I be yours, unless you are stripped of all self-will, both within and without? The sooner you do this, the better it will be for you; and if you do it with honesty and thoroughness, you will please me all the more, and gain all the more for yourself.

Some people surrender themselves but keep something back. They do not trust God utterly, but try to provide for themselves. Some at first offer all they have, but later on when temptations buffet them they take it back, and that is why they make no progress in goodness. These people will not attain the true liberty that belongs to the pure heart, or the grace of glad fellowship with me. They must first surrender themselves entirely, and every day offer self upon the altar. Without this the joyous union does not and cannot exist.

I have often said to you, and I say it again : Give up self, surrender yourself, and you will know great peace in your heart. Give your all for the one who is all; expect nothing, want nothing back; leave yourself with me wholly and without regrets, and you will possess me. You will be free in your heart, and the darkness will not bury you.[1] Strive towards this goal, make this your longing and your prayer—to be stripped of all possessions, and having nothing, to follow the Jesus who had nothing; to be dead to your own claims, and alive to me for ever.

Then all illusions will fade away, all unholy alarms, and all unnecessary cares. The fears that you cannot control will subside, the love you do not properly direct will perish.

[1] Ps. 138.11

XXXVIII

On being controlled where outward things are concerned, and on turning to God in danger

THE VOICE OF THE LORD : My son, you must resolutely aim at being inwardly free and your own master, in every place and in every outward deed and occupation. See that things are under you, not over you. Where your actions are concerned, be master and ruler, not slave or servant. Be a free man, a true Hebrew, transferred to the status and freedom of the sons of God, who stand above temporal things and spy out the eternal. They may observe what passes here, but they always keep one eye on the things of heaven. Temporal things do not rule their lives, because they make temporal things submit to the plan and purpose of God, the great craftsman who left nothing unplanned in all his creation.

In all that happens, you must not stop short at external appearances, or look at sights and sounds with human sense; on every occasion you must go at once with Moses into the Tabernacle, and ask the Lord's advice. Then you will often hear God's answer, and come back wiser to deal with present and future. Moses always had recourse to the Tabernacle when he had doubts and questions to settle; and to find relief from danger and the wickedness of men, he turned to the help of prayer. You likewise should take refuge in the inner room of your heart, earnestly imploring God's help. You read that Joshua and the people of Israel were deceived by the people of Gabaon because they

never asked the Lord for guidance first.[1] They were too
ready to believe fair words, and were tricked by a pre-
tence of friendship.

XXXIX

You must avoid over-anxiety

THE VOICE OF THE LORD : My son, always entrust your
concerns to me, and in due time I will arrange them to
your advantage. Wait for my decision, and you will
find it brings you profit.

THE DISCIPLE : Lord, I am very willing to entrust
everything to you, for my own thinking can do me little
good. If only I were not so concerned with the future,
but prepared to surrender myself without hesitation to
your good will!

THE LORD : My son, it often happens that a man feels a
desire for something and pursues it avidly; but once he
has achieved it, he begins to feel quite differently about
it. He never feels a lasting interest in anything, but is
always driven on from one thing to another. So it is
not unimportant to surrender your own will even in an
unimportant thing.

A man's true profit lies in renouncing his own self,
and the man who is so renounced is really free and
secure. But the ancient Enemy who sets himself against
all that is good never stops his tempting; day and night
he lays deep plots to see if he can catch someone off his
guard, and trip him headlong into the snare he has laid.

Watch and pray, says the Lord, *that you may not
enter into temptation.*[1]

[1] Jos. 9.14   [1] Matt. 26.41

XL

Man possesses no good thing of himself, and has nothing of which he can boast

THE DISCIPLE : Lord, *what is man that thou shouldst remember him? What is Adam's breed that it should claim thy care?*[1]

What has man done to earn the gift of your grace? Have I any reason to complain, Lord, if you abandon me? What plea can I offer in my defence[2] if you do not do what I ask? The right thing for me to think and say is this—Lord, I am nothing. I can do nothing. I possess nothing good of myself, but am deficient in everything, and my end is always nothing. Unless you aid and mould me inwardly, I am wholly cold and formless.

You, O Lord, are always the same; always and for ever you are still good and just and holy, directing all things in goodness, justice and holiness, and ordaining them in wisdom. I am more ready to go back than forward; I cannot keep myself from changing, for the seven seasons pass me by.[3] Yet my state improves the moment it pleases you to stretch out your hand to help me; for you alone without the aid of men can help and strengthen me, so that my face is sad no longer,[4] and my heart is turned and rests in you alone.

If I knew how to reject all the comfort the world can offer—whether I did so from longing for the state of devotion, or from the compulsion that drives me to seek you since no man can comfort me—then I might have

[1] Ps. 8.5   [2] Gen. 44.16
[3] Dan. 4.13   [4] I Kings 1.18

some reason to hope for your grace, and might rejoice in the gift of the new consolation.

Thanks be to you, when things go well with me, for all is sent by you.

Before you, I am a shadow and nothingness, a human creature, wavering and weak. What have I to boast of? why should I want to be well known? Can I boast of my nothingness? That would be utter foolishness— empty glorying is a curse and folly, because it draws us from the true glorying, and robs us of heavenly grace. As long as a man satisfies himself, he does not satisfy you. While he is gaping after the praise of men, he is cutting himself off from the real virtues.

True glorying and holy exultation is to glory in you, and not in oneself; to rejoice in your name, not in one's own powers; and to find delight in no created thing except for your sake. May your name be praised, not mine. May your works be exalted, not mine. May your holy name be blessed, and may none of men's praises ever be given to me. You are my glory, the rejoicing of my heart. In you will I glory and rejoice all the day long; but I will not boast of myself, except to tell of my humiliations.[5]

Let the Jews be content to receive honour from one another. I will be ambitious for the honour which comes from him who alone is God.[6] All the glory of men, all the honour of this world, all earthly rank, beside your eternal glory, are foolishness and unreality. O God, my truth, my mercy, O blessed Trinity, to you alone be blessing and honour and power and glory, throughout endless generations.[7]

[5] II Cor. 12.5   [6] John 5.44   [7] Apoc. 5.13

XLI

On despising worldly honour

THE VOICE OF THE LORD : My son, do not take it to heart
if you see others honoured and distinguished, while you
are passed over and left in obscurity. Lift up your
heart to me in heaven, and you will not be hurt by the
contempt of men on earth.

THE DISCIPLE : Lord, we are blind and easily deceived.
If I look at myself honestly, I can see that I have never
been wronged by any part of the creation, and so I
cannot justly bring you any complaint. I have sinned
often and grievously against you, and so it is only right
for the whole creation to take up arms against me.
Scorn and humiliation are my due, but praise and
honour and glory are yours.

Unless I prepare myself to be content when despised,
cast off and utterly disregarded by every living thing, I
cannot know inward peace and stability, receive spiritual enlightenment, or be made one with you.

XLII

You must not let your peace of mind depend on men

THE VOICE OF THE LORD : My son, if your peace is
dependent on some dear friend whose company gives
you pleasure, you will be insecure because you are
entangled; but if you turn at all times to the ever-
living, ever-abiding Truth, you will not be made unhappy if your friend leaves you or dies. Your love for
your friend must stand in me, and it is for my sake

that you must love any good man who is dear to you on earth. Friendship has no strength or lasting-power without me, and no affection that I have not joined can be pure and true.

You should be so dead to all such love and affection as to prefer, for your own part, to be free of all human companionship. A man approaches closer to God the further he withdraws from all earthly comfort. He also rises higher towards God as he sinks lower and becomes viler in his own eyes; anyone who credits himself with any good thing prevents the grace of God from appearing within him, for the grace of the Holy Spirit seeks a humble heart. If you knew how to annihilate self-interest and cast out all affection for the created world, then I would come, and my grace would well up abundantly within you. When you turn your eyes away towards created things you lose the vision of the Creator. Learn to overcome yourself in all things for the sake of the Creator, and so you will be able to attain to knowledge of God. However small a thing may be, if you are undisciplined enough to look back at it and love it, it will keep you from the highest good and bring a stain on your soul.

XLIII

Against the empty knowledge that this world offers

THE VOICE OF THE LORD: My son, you must not be impressed by men's fine words or subtle arguments. *It is power that builds up the kingdom of God, not words.*[1] Pay attention to the words I speak, for they inspire men's hearts and enlighten their minds; they induce compunction and bring all kinds of comfort with them.

[1] I Cor. 4.20

You must never read the Word in order to appear wiser or more learned. Concentrate on putting your failings to death, for this will do you more good than knowing many difficult questions. Even when you have read and learnt many things, you must still come back always to the one beginning.

It is I that *taught man all that man knows*,[2] and to my little ones I give a clearer understanding than any man can teach. The man to whom I speak will soon be wise and make great spiritual progress. How foolish people are when they go to men to learn about all kinds of unnecessary things, and give little thought to the way in which they can serve me. The time will come when Christ, the Lord of angels, shall appear, the masters' Master, who will hear the lessons of all and examine each man's conscience. Then the call will come for lamps, to search Jerusalem through.[3] What is hidden in darkness[4] shall then be revealed, and arguing tongues fall silent.

I am one that in a moment can raise the humble mind to more understanding of eternal truth than if he had given ten years to study. In my teaching there is no babble of words, no confusion of opinions, no arrogance of authority, no conflict of argument.

I am one that teaches a man to spurn the things of earth, and to loathe what is temporal; to seek the eternal and to relish the eternal; to shun honour and submit to slander; to rest all his hope in me, to desire nothing outside me, and to love me beyond all things with a burning love. There was once a man who loved me with all his heart, and he grasped divine mysteries and could speak wonderful things. He gained more by abandoning everything than by studying subtle theories.

To some I give a general message, to others I say things meant only for them; to certain people my sweet presence is known in signs and symbols, while to

[2] Ps. 93.10   [3] Sophon. 1.12   [4] I Cor. 4.5

a few I reveal mysteries in dazzling light. Books speak with one voice, but not everyone learns the same from them; for I am within a man, the Truth that teaches him—I search his heart, I know his thoughts, I advance his actions, and give to each man what I think he should have.

XLIV

On not interesting oneself in outward things

THE VOICE OF THE LORD : My son, you must remain in ignorance about many things, and consider yourself as one dead on this earth, to whom the world stands crucified.[1] There is much that you must pass through with deaf ears, keeping your mind on the things that bring you peace. It is better to turn away from things that annoy you, and to leave each man to his own opinions, than to be carried away in an argument. If you stand right with God, and keep his judgment in view, you will find it easier to let yourself be worsted.

THE DISCIPLE : Lord, what a state we have come to ! We lament any damage to our temporal interests and bustle about for some modest gain, while we forget any damage our souls have incurred, and hardly ever recall it. We give our attention to things that do us little or no good, and carelessly pass by the thing of supreme importance. The whole man tends to seep away to things outside, and unless he comes to his senses, he is soon content to lie submerged in externals.

[1] Gal. 6.14

XLV

We should not believe everybody; words are fallible things

THE DISCIPLE : O Lord, *it is thou that must deliver us from peril; vain is the help of man.*[1]

How often I have not found good faith where I thought it existed, and how often I have discovered it where I least expected! So it is useless to hope in men; but in you O God, there is salvation for the righteous. O Lord my God, may you be praised in all that happens to us.

We are weak and unstable, and it takes so little to change us and lead us astray. However carefully and cautiously a man tries to behave in every situation, he is bound to meet bewilderment and deception at some point. Yet the man who trusts you, O Lord, and seeks you in all sincerity will stand more firmly than most; and if trouble should come upon him, however inextricably he may seem to be involved, you will rescue him before long, or send him comfort—for you never fail the man who hopes in you to the end.

It is not often one finds a reliable friend who will be loyal in every kind of trouble. You O Lord, you alone are reliable in all things, and beside you there is no other like you.

How wise was the holy soul that said, My mind is solidly grounded and rooted in Christ.[2] If this were true of me, the fear of men would have less hold on me, and I would not mind so much what they say.

Is anyone capable of foreseeing everything or doing

[1] Ps. 59.13   [2] St Agatha

anything to avoid the evils he sees? The evils we do foresee still hurt us when they happen, so it is only to be expected that unforeseen ones will hurt us deeply too. But why did I not do more than I did to save myself this misery? and why was I so ready to believe what others said? We are still men with all the weaknesses of men, even if many people look on us as angels.

Is there anyone, Lord, I can believe? anyone but you? You are the Truth and you cannot deceive or be deceived. On the other hand, man's faith is false;[3] he is weak, unsteady and insecure, above all where the tongue is concerned; and so we can hardly believe anything straight away, even when it seems to be correct.

How wise you were to warn us not to put our trust in men,[4] telling us that a man's enemies will be the people of his own house,[5] and that if a man says, 'See here,' or 'See, he is there,'[6] we must not believe him.

Experience has taught me a lesson, and I hope it will bring more caution, not more folly. A man once said to me, 'Be careful—keep what I say to yourself.' And while I said nothing and thought that no one knew, he was unable to keep the very secret he had asked me to keep, but went his way, betraying both me and himself.

O Lord, protect me from careless speech and careless men like that; save me from falling into their clutches, or doing the same myself. Put true and trustworthy words in my mouth, and see that my tongue is never crafty. I must avoid doing at all costs what I do not want others to do to me.

What a good and peaceable thing it is if we can keep silent about other people, and not believe everything indiscriminately, or pass on what we have heard; if we

[3] Ps. 115.2   [4] Matt. 10.17
[5] Matt. 10.36   [6] Matt. 24.23

do not let everyone know our most intimate thoughts; if we are always seeking you, the Searcher of all hearts,[7] and are not driven before each new wind that blows,[8] but desire that all things, both within us and without, shall conform to your will and pleasure.

If we wish to keep the grace of heaven, the safest course is to shun all that is impressive in the eyes of the world, and instead of striving for the qualities that attract men's admiration, to spare no effort in developing those that bring fervour and amendment of life. We are very vulnerable in this life where all is testing and campaigning,[9] and harm has been done to many people when virtue was too quickly recognized and praised; but much benefit has come from grace that was fostered in silence.

XLVI

On having confidence in God when caught in a storm of hard words

THE VOICE OF THE LORD : My son, stand fast and put your hope in me. Words after all are only words— they fly through the air, but they do not hurt a stone. If you are guilty, say to yourself, ' I will gladly correct my faults'; if your conscience is clear, say, ' I am glad to bear this injustice for God's sake.' It is not much that you should sometimes bear hard words, seeing that you are not yet strong enough to endure hard blows.

The only reason why such little things cut you to the heart is that you are still ruled by your old nature, and take more notice of men than you should. It is because you are afraid of men's contempt that you are unwilling to be taken to task for your mistakes, and

[7] Prov. 24.12   [8] Eph. 4.14   [9] Job 7.1

try to cover them up with excuses. Look at yourself
carefully, and you will see that worldly interests are
still alive within you, as well as a foolish love of pleasing men. When you try to run away from the shame
and humiliation that result from wrong-doing, it is
quite clear that you have not learnt real humility, that
you are not really dead to the world, and that the world
does not stand crucified to you.[1]

Listen to my word, and you will not care about ten
thousand words of men. If everything that malice can
invent were said against you, what harm would it do
you, if you did not mind in the slightest and let it all
pass by? Could it pull a single hair from your head?

A man is easily upset by censure when he does not
keep his thoughts centred within him and his eyes fixed
on God; but the man who trusts in me and does not
attempt to stand by his own judgment will be free from
the fear of men. I am the Judge from whom no secret
is hidden[2]—I am aware how each deed is done; I know
who commits a wrong and who has to bear it. I
allowed that word to be said; that thing was done with
my permission. *And so the thoughts of many hearts
shall be made manifest.*[3] I shall judge both innocent
and guilty; but first of all it is my pleasure to test them
both in secret. What men say about a person is often
false, but my judgment is true—it will stand firm and
not be reversed. Mostly it is concealed, and few know
all its details; but it never makes a mistake, nor can it
make a mistake, even if it seems unjust to those who
have no wisdom.

Whenever judgment is passed, you must flee to me
and not make your own decisions; for God will not let
anything befall the just man to do him hurt.[4] And so
he will not greatly care even if some unjust charge is
brought against him; on the other hand, he will not be
foolishly pleased even if others excuse him and find him

[1] Gal. 6.14   [2] Dan. 13.42   [3] Luke 2.35   [4] Prov. 12.21

justified. He reminds himself that I am *one who probes the innermost heart*,[5] that I do not judge by appearances,[6] or the things for which men have eyes—often a thing that men judge praiseworthy is in my eyes worthy of blame.

THE DISCIPLE : O Lord God, judge ever true,[7] who know the weakness and the wickedness of men, be my strength and all my confidence, for my own knowledge is not enough for me. You know what I do not know, and so I should humble myself and bear it with mildness when fault is found with me. Be gracious and forgive me for all the times I have not done so, and once more grant me the grace to submit. For it is better to leave it to your abundant mercy to grant me pardon, than to assert my fancied righteousness and stifle my secret sense of guilt. Even if *my conscience does not reproach me, that is not where my justification lies*;[8] for without the action of your mercy, *what man is there living that can stand guiltless in thy presence*?[9]

XLVII

Every hardship is worth enduring for the sake of eternal life

THE VOICE OF THE LORD : My son, you must not let yourself be crushed under the labours you have undertaken for my sake, nor utterly downcast by the difficult things that come your way; whatever happens, let my promise strengthen and encourage you. I am sufficient to reward you beyond all measuring and all limit. Your toil here will not last long, and you will not always be

[5] Apoc. 2.23   [6] John 7.24   [7] Ps. 7.12
[8] I Cor. 4.4   [9] Ps. 142.2

weighed down with sorrows. Wait just a while, and you will soon see an end to your troubles. A time will come when all your toil and struggling will cease; and anything that passes away with time is brief and unimportant.

Go on with what you are doing. Work faithfully in my vineyard, and I shall be your reward. Write, read and sing; lament your sins, keep silence, pray; bravely endure all that you find hard to bear—eternal life is worth all these and greater struggles too. Peace will come to you on a day which is already known to the Lord, and then there will be no day or night such as you know on this earth, but perpetual light, splendour without end, peace that cannot be broken, calm that holds no fear. You will not then say, *Who is to set me free from a nature thus doomed to death?*[1] nor will you cry, *Unhappy I, that live an exile in Mosoch;*[2] for *death shall be engulfed,*[3] and salvation be complete. Then there will be no fear, but blessed joy and sweet companionship, full of pure delight.

If only you had once seen the unfading crowns of the saints in heaven, the great glory that fills with joy those who once were thought of no account in the eyes of the world, not worthy even to live! Then you would certainly humble yourself to the ground, and would strive to be the servant of all rather than the master of one. You would not desire days of happiness in this life, but would rejoice to endure hardships for God's sake; and you would think you had gained most when you counted least among men. If you relished these things and they really had a meaning in your heart, would you dare to utter a single complaint? Surely every hardship is worth enduring for the sake of eternal life? It is no trivial matter to win or lose God's kingdom. So lift your face to heaven—there I am, and

[1] Rom. 7.24   [2] Ps. 119.5   [3] Is. 25.8

with me are all those saints of mine who faced a hard struggle in this world. Now they rejoice, now they are comforted, now they know peace and rest; and they shall remain with me in my Father's kingdom for ever.

XLVIII

On the eternal day, and this life's anguish

THE DISCIPLE : Blessed home in the city above! Eternity's bright day that night never shadows, filled with light ever streaming from the Truth supreme; day for ever glad, for ever free from fear, constant and unchanging! If only that day had dawned and all that belongs to this life had drawn to its end! For the saints, that day shines glorious with never-fading splendour, but for the wanderers on this earth there is only a distant reflection. The citizens of heaven know the joys of that day, but the exiled sons of Eve can only mourn the bitterness and weariness of this.

The days of our existence in time are brief and evil, full of anguish and pain. Here man is stained by sin, ensnared by passion, gripped by fear and torn by care; here he is distracted by so many unimportant things, involved in so many pointless activities, surrounded by so many chances of going wrong; he is worn down by hardship, burdened by temptation, weakened by pleasure, and tormented by want.

When will these troubles come to an end? When shall I be freed from the wretchedness of slavery to sin? When shall I think of you alone, O God, find all my joy in you? When shall I shake off all that hinders me, escape the burden of body and mind, and be really free? When shall I know continuous peace, peace that cannot be disturbed or shaken, peace within and without, peace built firm on every side? Good Jesus, when

shall I stand and gaze on you, when shall I behold the
glory of your kingdom? When will you be all in all to
me? O when shall I be with you in the kingdom you
have kept prepared for those you love from all eternity?[1] Here I am on a hostile earth, a poor abandoned
exile, amid daily warfare, suffering great distress.

Comfort me in my exile, and ease my suffering—my
every longing sighs for you, and all the comfort of this
world is nothing but a burden.

I long to have the joy of you in my inmost heart, but
I cannot find you. I yearn to hold fast to heavenly
things, but temporal interests and the longings I have
not killed drag me down again. My spirit desires to
rise above all things, yet my natural instincts keep me
subject against my will. *Pitiable creature that I am,*[2] *I*
am at war with myself, and my life has become a burden
to me;[3] for my spirit yearns for heaven, but my old
nature prefers the earth. What suffering this means!—
just when my mind is filled with thoughts of heaven, a
host of worldly thoughts bursts in upon my prayer.

O God, do not keep your distance from me.[4] Do not
turn away from your servant in anger. Brandish your
lightnings to rout my enemies; shoot your arrows, and
throw into confusion[5] all the phantoms the Enemy
marshals against me. Gather every thought into still-
ness before you; make me forget everything that belongs
to the world, and enable me to scorn and reject the
imaginings of sin. Celestial sweetness, come to help me,
and let every impurity flee from your face.

Forgive me, and in your mercy pardon me, whenever
I think of anything in my prayers but you. For I must
confess that I have grown used to letting my thoughts
be distracted. Very often I am not where my body sits
or stands—I am where my imagination takes me. I am
where my thoughts are, and my thoughts are often

---

[1] Matt. 25.34   [2] Rom. 7.24   [3] Job 7.20
[4] Ps. 70.12   [5] Ps. 143.6

where the thing I love is. My mind is filled with things that are naturally attractive, or that I have grown fond of from habit. You are the Truth, and you told us plainly: *Where your treasure-house is, there your heart is too.*[6] If it is heaven that I love, I am glad to think of heavenly things. If it is the world I am attached to, then I rejoice with the world's happiness, and am saddened by its misfortunes. If I am attached to the body, I let my thoughts dwell on the things that interest the body; if I love the spirit, I delight to think of spiritual things. It is the things I love that I gladly speak and think about; it is thoughts of these things that I carry home with me.

Yet that man is really happy who, for your sake, Lord, can say farewell to all created things, and do violence to his natural longings, and by the burning desire of his spirit, crucify the corrupt desires of the flesh. Then from a conscience that is at peace, he can offer you pure prayer, and be fit to stand among the angelic choir, body and soul oblivious of earthly things.

XLIX

On desiring the everlasting life, and on the great rewards promised to those who fight manfully

THE VOICE OF THE LORD: My son, at times you are conscious of a longing for the eternal blessedness pouring into your heart from above. You are eager to leave the brief dwelling place of the body,[1] so that you can look full at my glory where no shifting shadow dims it. Open up your heart then, and with all the longing in you drink in this holy inspiration. Offer abundant thanks to the goodness of heaven that deals so graciously

<hr>

[6] Matt. 6.21   [1] II Peter 1.13

with you, that visits you in mercy, stirs and kindles your soul, and mightily bears you up lest your own weight drag you back to earth. You do not receive this gift by any aims and efforts of your own, but purely out of the graciousness of heaven's favour and the divine consideration for you, so that you may make progress in goodness and humility, prepare yourself for future struggles, and long with all the affection of your heart to stay close beside me and serve me with willing fervour.

My son, when a fire is alight, the flames leap up, but there is often smoke as well. In the same way, there is in some people a flame of desire for heavenly things, yet they are not free from the temptation of worldly longings. So the petitions they offer so earnestly to God are not solely concerned with bringing honour to his name. Your own desires which you say are so urgent are often impure like this; for nothing can be pure and perfect when it is tinged with self-interest. Do not ask for what you find delightful and convenient, but for what pleases and honours me; for if your values are right, you should prefer my command to your own desires, and seek my will rather than anything you have set your heart on.

I know what you yearn for. I have heard your sighs of longing. You would like to be in the glorious freedom of God's sons now.[2] You already find delight in the thought of the everlasting home and the heavenly country where all is gladness; but that hour has not yet come—another time is still with you, the time of fighting, the time of toil and testing. You desire to be filled with the great good, but you cannot have it now —I am he; wait for me, says the Lord, *till the kingdom of God has come.*[3]

You still have to be tested and exercised in many

[2] Rom. 8.21   [3] Luke 22.18

points here on earth. You will receive comfort sometimes, but you cannot have full contentment. So keep
your courage high and play the man,[4] both in doing
and enduring what goes against the grain. You must
be clothed in the new self,[5] turned into a new man.[6]
You must often do things for which you have no inclination, and give up other things that you want to do.
The things that please other people will go well, what
pleases you will make no progress. What others say
will be heard with attention, what you say will be
thought worthless. Others will ask and will receive,
you will ask and get nothing. Others will be much
spoken of and praised, you will be passed over in
silence. Others will be entrusted with one task or
another, but you will be thought good for nothing.
Your old nature will sometimes find this painful, and it
is a great thing if you can endure it in silence. It is in
situations like this that the faithful servant of the Lord
is tested in his ability to deny his own nature and
utterly crush his own inclinations.

Your old self needs to be put to death most of all
perhaps at those times when you have to see and
submit to something that you do not like, especially
when you are ordered to do inconvenient things that
do not seem very useful. Since you are a man under
authority, it is a question of not daring to resist the
power set over you, and so you find it hard to give up
all right to your own opinions and live your life at
another's beck and call.

But think of the harvest from these labours, my son;
think of the end that will soon come, and the very
great reward to follow—then you will not feel any
burden, but will experience strong comfort in your
patience. For in place of this insignificant will of yours
which you now resign of your own accord, you will

⁴ Josh. 1.7   ⁵ Eph. 4.24   ⁶ I Kings 10.6

have your will in heaven always. There you will find everything you want, everything you can desire. There all that is good will be yours to have, without fear of ever losing it. There your will, for ever one with mine, will desire nothing for itself, nothing to which I am stranger. There no one will stand in your way, no one complain of you; no one will hinder you, nothing will be an obstacle; but all you long for will be granted in a moment, and all your desires be completely satisfied and fulfilled. There in return for the humiliation you have endured, I will give you glory, and you that went sorrowing shall be gaily clad.[7] Instead of the lowest place, you shall have a throne in the kingdom for ever. There you will reap the harvest of your obedience; the drudgery of penitence will be rewarded with joy, and your humble submission win a glorious crown.

So in this present life submit in humble obedience to all; do not care who it was who said this or gave that order, but take great care that whether it is a superior, a subordinate or an equal who makes a request or gives you an order, you receive it all in good part and endeavour to carry it out in simple goodwill. Let other people set their hearts on all kinds of things, let others boast of this or that and receive their countless praises—your boast must lie in rejecting self and seeking my will and honour. The one thing you must desire is that in life or in death, you may bring glory to God.[8]

[7] Is. 61.3   [8] Phil. 1.20

L

The man who is deprived of spiritual peace should entrust himself to the hands of God

THE DISCIPLE : O Lord God, blessings on your name now and for ever, because what you will has been done, and what you do is good. May your servant find his joy in you, not in himself or any other. You alone are my true gladness; you are my hope and my reward, you, Lord, my joy and honour. Your servant has no powers that did not come by gift from you,[1] without any merit on his part. All is yours, both what you have given and what you have made.

Ever since youth, misery and mortal sickness have been my lot,[2] and sometimes my soul is so troubled that it weeps; the sufferings that surround it fill it with dismay. I long to know the joy of peace; I cry out for the peace that comes to your sons when they are fed by your hand in the brightness of spiritual solace. If you grant peace, if you shower that holy joy upon me, the soul of your servant will be filled with melody, and he will devotedly sing your praise; but if you withdraw yourself as you so often do, he will not find easy the path you have decreed.[3] Rather he will fall on his knees and beat his breast because things are no longer as they were before, when your light shone above him[4] and he was hidden under the shelter of your wings[5] from the temptations that set upon him.

Righteous Father, ever worthy of praise, the hour has come when your servant is to be tested. Beloved

[1] I Cor. 4.7   [2] Ps. 87.16   [3] Ps. 118.32
[4] Job 29.3   [5] Ps. 16.8

Father, it is right that your servant should at this hour
endure something for your sake. Father for ever to
be worshipped, the hour has come which you foresaw
from endless ages past would come, when the world
should think for a time that your servant had been
destroyed, though in your sight his inward life never
falters. Let him be sneered at for a while, let him be
crushed and humiliated in the sight of men, let him
be broken by suffering and exhaustion; for then he will
rise again with you in the dawn of the new day, and
be filled with glory in the heavenly places.

Holy Father, this was your command, your will;
what you decreed has come to pass. When I am asked
to endure suffering and trouble in this world for love of
you, however frequent it may be and whatever its cause,
I count it as a favour shown by you to a friend. Without your counsel and foreknowledge nothing happens on
this earth: *never was ill without a cause.*[6] *It was in
mercy thou didst chasten me, schooling me to thy obedience,*[7] so that I might discard all the arrogance and
presumption of my heart. It was good for me to blush
with confusion,[8] so that I should look to you for comfort rather than to men. This has taught me to tremble
at your inscrutable verdict, for you strike the godly
man along with the ungodly, yet still you are righteous
and just.

I thank you for not being lenient with my evil ways,
but wearing me down with bitter blows, inflicting sorrows on me, and sending distresses within and without.
Of all that exist beneath the heaven there is no one to
comfort me, but you O Lord my God, the soul's
divine physician; it is yours to smite and to heal,[9] yours
to bring men to the grave and to bring them back
again.[10] Your rod is over me and your discipline shall
teach me.

[6] Job 5.6   [7] Ps. 118.71   [8] Ps. 68.8
[9] Deut. 32.39   [10] Tob. 13.2; I Kings 2.6

Beloved Father, I am in your hands. I submit to your chastening rod. Strike my neck and my back, so that I may straighten out my crooked ways and bend myself to your will. Make me your loving humble disciple, as you know so well how to do; and then I will direct my steps in obedience to your slightest wish. I commit to your correction myself and all that is mine, for it is better to be called to account in this life than in the one to come.

You are aware of all things, every single thing; nothing in the conscience of man can escape your notice. You know what is coming before it happens, and you do not need anyone to tell you what men are doing on earth. You know what will help me to progress, and how the rust of sin can be cleaned off by suffering. Carry out your desire and pleasure with me, and do not scorn my poor sinful existence, which you know more fully and clearly than anyone.

Grant, O Lord, that I may know what I ought to know, and love what I ought to love; that I may praise what most pleases you, value what is precious in your eyes, and reject what you find vile.

Do not leave me to judge by appearances, or to base my opinions on the ignorant rumours of men,[11] but give me discernment and right judgment in earthly and spiritual matters, and help me to set your will and your good pleasure above all things. Men's senses are fallible and often lead to false judgments, and lovers of this world are misled by their exclusive passion for visible things. Does it make a man any better to be thought highly of by men? When one man praises another, one deceiver is misled by another, one fool by another, the blind by the blind, and the weak by the weak; and this empty praise will really make a man look foolish in the end; for, as the humble Saint Francis

[11] Is. 11.3

said, 'A man is what he appears in God's eyes, and not the slightest bit more.'

LI

You must press on with humble works when you fall short of the highest ones

THE VOICE OF THE LORD : My son, you cannot keep up a really fervent longing for goodness, nor spend all your time on the heights of contemplation. The essential sinfulness of your nature means that you must come down from time to time to lower things, and submit to the burden of mortal life in spite of your unwillingness and loathing. As long as you wear a mortal body you will know restlessness and a heavy heart. While you live in the flesh, the burden of the flesh will prove a sorrow to you, for it will not let you devote yourself to spiritual thoughts and contemplation of God without interruption.

At such times it is best for you to turn to lowlier outward activities, and refresh your soul in good works, confidently waiting for me to come and visit you from on high, and bear your exile and the dryness of your soul with patience, until I come to you again and you are freed from all your anxieties. For I will make you forget your unhappiness and grant you peace in your heart. I will spread out before you the green fields of the Scriptures, so that your heart is opened wide, and the path I have decreed lies easy before you.[1] And then you will say, *Not that I count these present sufferings as the measure of that glory which is to be revealed in us.*[2]

[1] Ps. 118.32   [2] Rom. 8.18

LII

A man should consider himself unworthy of any spiritual comfort and fit only for punishment

THE DISCIPLE : Lord, I am not worthy to receive your comfort, or any spiritual visitation—you treat me as I deserve when you leave me helpless and alone. If I could weep an ocean of tears I would still be unworthy of your comfort. I deserve nothing but torture and punishment, because I have so deeply and so often offended you, and sinned so grievously on so many occasions. If a true account is rendered, I am found unworthy of the slightest comfort.

But you, O God, are merciful and compassionate, and do not wish your works to perish, but intend rather to display in those who are objects of your mercy how rich your goodness is.[1] Your servant can never deserve it, and yet you grant him comfort beyond all human measure, for your comfort is utterly unlike the words that men can offer.

What have I done, Lord, to deserve any heavenly comfort? As far as I can recall, I have not done anything good, but have always been ready to sin and slow to mend my ways. That is the truth and I cannot deny it. If I were to say anything else, you would stand there against me, and there would be no one to defend me. What I deserve for my sins is hell and everlasting fire. I honestly confess that I have earned every kind of scorn and insult, and am not fit to be named among those who follow you devoutly. I do not like hearing this, yet for truth's sake, I will accuse myself and blame my own wrongdoing; then it will be easier for me to

[1] Rom. 9.23

194

win your mercy. I am guilty and covered with confusion; what can I say? There is nothing I can say but this : I have sinned, O Lord, I have sinned; have mercy on me and forgive me. *For a little leave me to myself, to find some comfort in my misery. Soon I must go to a land of darkness, death's shadow over it.*[2]

The one thing that you ask of the guilty miserable sinner is repentance and shame for his sins. For where there is true repentance and humbling of the heart, hope of mercy is born; the troubled conscience finds peace, lost grace is restored, man is saved from the vengeance that draws near,[3] and God meets the penitent soul with a loving holy kiss.

O Lord, when the humble repentance of sinners is offered up before you, you take pleasure in the sacrifice; its perfume is sweeter than incense as it rises up before you. This is the precious ointment that you wished to have poured on your holy feet,[4] for a heart that is humbled and contrite you have never disdained.[5] There is the place of refuge from our enemy's furious glance; there is the place where every mark and stain is cleansed and washed away.

LIII

The grace of God cannot be combined with worldly-mindedness

THE VOICE OF THE LORD : My son, my grace is a precious thing—it cannot be combined with outward interests and earthly comforts. If you want to receive grace, you must throw aside everything that will stand in its way.

Find a secret place for yourself, and make it your delight to spend your time there alone. Instead of talk-

[2] Job 10.20-21   [3] Luke 3.7
[4] *v.* John 12.3-7   [5] Ps. 50.19

ing to other people, pour out to God your prayers of devotion; then you will keep your heart repentant and your conscience clear. Let the whole world be valueless to you, and above every external thing put the need to be free for God. You cannot be free for me and at the same time be finding delight in things that pass away. You have to separate yourself from those you know and love, and keep your heart free of all the comfort of this world. That is why the blessed Apostle Peter calls upon Christ's faithful followers to be like strangers and exiles in this world, and to keep themselves apart.[1]

A man can die with confidence when no links of affection bind him to this world; but the spirit that is sick cannot keep the heart detached from everything like that, and the natural man is incapable of understanding the freedom the spiritual man enjoys. Yet if he really desires to be a spiritual man, he has to renounce every human claim, distant or near, and be on his guard against no one so much as himself. If you have conquered yourself, you will find it easier to overcome other things. It is the triumph over one's own nature that means full victory; for when a man has himself under control so that every desire submits to reason and reason submits to me, then he is really victorious over self, and is master of the world.

If you aspire to scale such heights, you must make a bold beginning; lay the axe to the root, and tear out that secret undisciplined inclination for your own will and anything that promises material personal benefits. Man is far too uncontrolled in love of self, and you will find that this fault is the cause of nearly everything that needs to be uprooted and destroyed. Once self-love has been subdued and conquered, you will know great peace and quietness.

Very few people make any effort to die completely
[1] I Peter 2.11

to their own interests, and they do not try wholeheartedly to leave themselves behind. This is why they
remain tied up in their own natures and cannot be
raised above themselves in spirit. If a man desires to
walk in liberty with me, it is essential that he put to
death all his sinful and undisciplined emotions and no
longer cling to any created thing with longing or affection.

LIV

The different effects of nature and grace

THE VOICE OF THE LORD : My son, you must carefully
observe the effects of nature and of grace, because they
operate very differently, and the subtle distinction between them can only be marked by an enlightened and
spiritual man. Everyone aims at what is good and
makes some pretension to it in his words and actions.
That is why many people are deceived by an imitation
of goodness.

Nature is cunning; it misleads people and tricks and
deceives them, and always has its own interest at heart.
But grace walks honestly and openly; it avoids all that
has a look of evil about it,[1] and it lays no traps; it does
everything solely for the sake of God, in whom it finds
its ultimate rest.

Nature is not prepared to be put to death, or to be
subdued and overcome. It does not want to be under
control or to submit of its own free will. But grace
aims at putting the old nature to death, and it resists
the desires of the body. It is eager to submit, and longs
to be ruled. It does not want to be independent, but
loves to be under discipline. It has no wish to lord it
over anyone, but is prepared to live its whole life and

[1] I Thess. 5.22

spend its whole existence subject to the will of God; and for love of the Lord to submit humbly to every kind of human authority.[2]

Nature labours for its own good, and looks to see what advantage it can get from somebody else; but grace does not consider its personal convenience and advantage, but rather what will do most good to others.

Nature is always ready to accept respect and honour, but grace faithfully attributes all honour and glory to God.

Nature is afraid of humiliation and contempt, but grace rejoices when it *suffers indignity for the sake of Jesus' name.*[3]

Nature likes idleness and physical ease, but grace cannot endure to be unoccupied, and gladly undertakes all kinds of toil.

Nature is eager to possess rare and beautiful things, and loathes common and coarse ones. But grace finds its delight in what is simple and humble; it is not repulsed by the repulsive, and it does not refuse to put on worn out clothes.

Nature has its eye on temporal things, and is pleased by worldly advantage. It is unhappy when it suffers loss, and any slighting word can make it angry. But grace is concerned with eternal things, and has no interest in anything temporal. In material loss it feels no distress, and when hard things are said it feels no resentment, for its treasure and its joy are laid up in heaven where nothing ever is lost.[4]

Nature is greedy, and is more ready to receive than give. It loves exclusive, unshared things. Grace is loving and generous; it rejects private advantage, and is content with little, thinking it *more blessed to give than to receive.*[5]

Nature inclines to material things and gratification of

2 I Peter 2.13   3 Acts 5.41
4 Matt. 6.19-20   5 Acts 20.35

self, towards useless pastimes and travelling about. Grace gravitates towards God and goodness; it renounces material things, and tries to avoid the world. It loathes the longings of the body; it curbs the desire to wander abroad, and hates the thought of appearing in public.

Nature likes to experience outside comforts which bring satisfaction to the senses; but grace seeks its comfort in God alone, and beyond all visible things it looks to the Supreme Good for its delight.

Nature does everything for its own gain and advantage. It cannot do anything for nothing, but is always hoping for something as good or better, some praise or favour, in return for its good deeds. It wants anything it does or gives or says to be appreciated. Grace does not look for anything in this world, and it asks for no reward but God. It only wants the necessities of this life in so far as they help it to win eternal life.

Nature is pleased when it has many friends and associates. It glories in high place and noble birth; it smiles on the powerful, flatters the rich, and applauds those like itself. But grace loves even its enemies, and is not pleased with itself when it has a crowd of friends. It thinks nothing of position or high birth unless there is goodness there as well. It favours the poor rather than the rich, and feels more sympathy with the innocent than with the powerful. It *rejoices at the victory of truth,*[6] not falsehood; and it is always urging men to *prize the best gifts of heaven,*[7] and to grow more like the Son of God in goodness.

Nature is quick to complain of want and difficulty, but grace bears hardship without giving way.

Nature diverts everything to its own ends, it struggles and argues on its own account. Grace leads everything home to God, the source from whom it comes. It does not credit itself with anything good or make any arro-

[6] I Cor. 13.6   [7] I Cor. 12.31

gant claims; it is not pushing, it does not force its views on others; but whatever it feels, whatever it thinks, it submits itself to the eternal wisdom and the scrutiny of God.

Nature is always eager to know secrets and hear news. It wants to go out into the world and have all kinds of experiences. It longs to be recognized and do things that earn praise and admiration. Grace has no interest in hearing new strange things, because all this springs from our age-old corruption, and there can be nothing new or lasting here on this earth.[8]

Grace teaches a man to keep his senses in check, to avoid empty complacency and ostentation, and to conceal in humility all that might be praised and admired; and from all that happens and in all he learns, it teaches him to seek the harvest of usefulness and the praise and the glory of God. Grace does not want itself or its doings talked about, but it does want God to be blessed where all his gifts are concerned, for he sends all his gifts purely out of love.

Grace like this is a supernatural light, a special gift of God; it is the seal of the elect, and a pledge of eternal salvation. It raises a man from earthly things to love of heavenly ones, and it makes him spiritual where he was unspiritual before.

As nature is curbed and subdued, grace flows in more richly, and the inward man is visited anew, and daily remade in the image of God.

[8] Eccles. 1.9

LV

On the corruption of nature and the efficacy of divine grace

THE DISCIPLE: O Lord God, who created me in your image and your likeness, grant me this wonderful grace which is so necessary for my salvation, so that I may overcome this evil nature of mine which draws me away to sin and destruction. For I am conscious of a disposition towards sin in my lower self, which goes against the disposition of my conscience and hands me over captive,[1] so that I do as my body commands. I am powerless to withstand its longings without the help of your holy grace burning within my heart.

I need your grace, and I need so much of it, if I am to overcome nature which *even in youth is so bent towards evil*.[2] For through the first man, Adam, nature fell and was spoiled by sin, and every man has inherited the penalty of that stain. When you created nature, it was good and upright, yet by 'nature' we now mean 'the faultiness and weakness of corrupt nature'; for when it is left to itself, every impulse it feels is for the lower and the bad. Some feeble powers have survived, like a spark hidden under the ashes, for natural reason still exists. Thick darkness surrounds it, yet it can still judge good and bad, and distinguish true and false. But it is not strong enough to put into effect what it knows is good, because it no longer has the full light of truth, and its former healthy affections.

The result of all this is that inwardly I applaud your disposition, O God[3]—I know that your command is

[1] Rom. 7.23   [2] Gen. 8.21   [3] Rom. 7.22

holy, right and good,[4] and I realize I must flee all sin and evil; but *my natural powers are at the disposition of sin,*[5] and so I obey my body rather than my mind. That is why *praiseworthy intentions are always ready to hand, but I cannot find my way to the performance of them.*[6] That is why I am always making good resolutions, but if there is no grace to help my weakness, I retreat and give in to the slightest opposition. That is why I recognize the path to perfection, and see clearly enough how I should behave, but the burden of my wicked nature weighs me down, and I cannot rise to better things.

O Lord, I need your grace so much if I am to start anything good, or go on with it, or bring it to completion. Without grace, I have no power to do anything—but nothing is beyond my powers, if your grace gives strength to me.[7]

True grace of heaven! Without it, personal achievement and natural gifts are worthless. Without grace, riches and skills, beauty and strength, intellect and eloquence, carry no weight, O Lord, with you. For natural gifts are common to good and bad alike, but grace or divine love is the special gift of the elect. It is a mark set upon them that gives them fitness for eternal life, and so important is it, that without it the gift of prophecy, the working of miracles and deep speculation all count for nothing. Not even faith and hope and other virtues are acceptable to you if charity and grace are not there also.

Blessed grace! You make the poor in spirit rich in goodness, and the rich man you make humble in his heart. Come down to me, and pour out your comfort on me soon, or my soul will faint from weariness and dryness.

[4] Rom. 7.12   [5] Rom. 7.25   [6] Rom. 7.18   [7] Phil. 4.13

Lord, I beseech you to look on me in mercy, for your grace is enough for me,[8] if I am denied the things that nature desires. If I am tempted and troubled by misfortunes, I will not fear any harm while your grace is with me. For your grace is my strength, and it brings help and counsel. It is stronger than any enemy, and wiser than all the wise. It teaches a man the truth, and guides him in discipline; it gives light to the heart, brings comfort in distress and puts sorrow to flight; it takes away fears, nourishes devotion, and induces tears of repentance. Without grace I am dead wood, a useless stump, fit only for throwing away.

So, Lord, may your grace always go behind and before me, and enable me to devote myself continually to good works, through Jesus Christ, your son. Amen.

LVI

We must reject the claims of self and follow Christ's example through the cross

THE VOICE OF THE LORD : My son, you can only enter into my being as you escape from your own. It is when you desire nothing from the world outside that inward peace will be yours; and it is when you give up self in your inmost thoughts that union with God will become a reality.

It is my will for you to learn complete denial of self, accepting my will without rebellion or complaint.

Follow me—*I am the way; I am truth and life.*[1] Without the way, there is no travelling, without the truth, no knowing, without the life, no living. I am the way you must follow, the truth you must believe, the

[8] II Cor. 12.9   [1] John 14.6

life you must hope for. I am the way that cannot go astray, the truth that cannot mislead, the life that cannot end. I am the straightest way, the highest truth; I am the true life, the blessed life, the uncreated life. If you keep to my way, *you will come to know the truth, and the truth will set you free,*[2] and then you will lay your grasp on eternal life.[3]

If you have a mind to enter into life, keep the commandments.[4] If you have a mind to know the truth, believe in me. If you have a mind to be perfect, sell all you have.[5] If you have a mind to become my follower, renounce yourself.[6] If you have a mind to be exalted in heaven, make yourself humble on earth. If you have a mind to share my kingdom, carry the cross with me; for it is only the servants of the cross that find the way of blessedness and true light.

THE DISCIPLE : Lord Jesus, your way was narrow and despised in this world. Grant that I may follow in your steps amidst the world's contempt, for *a disciple is no better than his master, a servant than his lord.*[7]

Let your life exercise all your servant's thinking, for it is there that my salvation and my true holiness lies. Nothing else I read or hear can refresh me or bring me real delight.

THE LORD : My son, you have read all this and know it —you will be blessed if you put it into practice. *The man who loves me is the man who keeps the commandments he has from me. . . . I will love him, and will reveal myself to him,*[8] and will make him sit beside me in the kingdom of my Father.

THE DISCIPLE : Lord Jesus, grant that I may one day know this promise fulfilled in my life. I have taken up my cross, I have taken it from your hand. I will carry

[2] John 8.32   [3] I Tim. 6.12   [4] Matt. 19.17
[5] Matt. 19.21   [6] Matt. 16.24   [7] Matt. 10.24
[8] John 14.21

it, and carry it till my death, in obedience to the command you have laid on me. How true it is that 'The good monk's life is all a cross, but it leads the way to Paradise.'[9] I have undertaken this thing, and I may not turn back or give up my purpose.

Come then, my brothers, we must press on together, for Jesus will be with us. It is for Jesus' sake that we have taken up this cross—for Jesus' sake we must go on with it. We have a leader who marches at our head, and he will help us. Look! It is our King that goes before us, and he will fight for us. Let us follow boldly, none of us afraid, every one of us ready to die in battle. We must never *suffer any foul blot to fall on our name*[10] by drawing back from the cross.

LVII

A warning against excessive dejection when life seems to go wrong

THE VOICE OF THE LORD : My son, I am more pleased to see patience and humility when things are difficult, than a state of devotion and spiritual joy when all goes well.

Why let yourself be made unhappy by some little thing said against you? Even if it had been a bigger thing, it should not have disturbed you. As it is, let it pass. It is nothing new, and it is not the first occasion; and if you live for any length of time, it will not be the last.

[9] From 'Lines on the Holy Cross', one of Thomas à Kempis's 'Spiritual Songs'.
[10] I Macc. 9.10

You are strong enough, as long as nothing difficult comes your way. You are also good at giving advice, and you know how to speak words of comfort to others; but when an unexpected trouble comes knocking at your door, your strength and advice disappear. You must give your attention to your own weakness, which is often enough revealed to you when you face quite little problems. All the same, this sort of thing is sent to help your salvation.

Whatever the trouble, put it out of your heart as best you can; even if it does touch you, do not let it depress you or keep you concerned for too long. If you cannot bear it joyfully, bear it patiently at least. Even if it makes you angry and indignant, restrain your feelings. Do not allow past your lips any uncontrolled word that will hurt the conscience of my little ones. All the commotion that has been stirred up will soon die away, and your inward pain will be turned to sweetness by the renewal of grace. I am still living, says the Lord, and I am ready to help you and comfort you more than you have ever known, if you trust me and call on me devoutly.

Take things more calmly, and brace yourself to endure things better. Everything is not ruined if you often find yourself in difficulty and facing strong temptation. You are man, not God. You are a mortal creature, not an angel. How could you possibly maintain an unchanging state of virtue when it proved impossible for the angels in heaven and Adam in Paradise? It is mine to comfort the mourner with new hope,[1] and it is those that know their own weakness that I raise to my divinity.

THE DISCIPLE : Lord, blessings on what you have said. It is sweeter to my taste than honey dripping from its

[1] Job 5.11

comb.[2] What should I do in all these troubles and difficulties without the comfort of your holy words? Provided that one day I reach the harbour of salvation, what do I care how much I suffer first? Grant me a good end. Grant me a happy passage from this world. Remember me, O my God, and guide me by a straight path to your kingdom. Amen.

LVIII

On not prying into the secrets of God's judgments or other exalted things

THE VOICE OF THE LORD: My son, beware of arguing about deep questions and the secrets of God's judgments. Do not discuss why one man is left to himself while another is accepted into such a state of grace; why one man suffers so much and another is advanced in every way. Things like this are beyond man's understanding, and no reasoning or discussion can find the answer where the judgments of God are concerned.

So if the Enemy suggests it to you, or if you find men being curious and asking this sort of question, reply in the words of the prophet: *So just, Lord, thou art, thy awards so truly given.*[1] Or this: *How unerring are the awards which the Lord makes, one and all giving proof of their justice!*[2] My judgments are to be feared, not discussed, for they are incomprehensible to man.

Besides this, do not investigate or discuss the merits of the saints, arguing which one is holiest or greatest in the kingdom of heaven. Such questions are often the cause of quarrelling and useless argument. They encourage pride and empty boasting, and these in turn

[2] Ps. 18.11; Ps. 118.103   [1] Ps. 118.137   [2] Ps. 18.10

give rise to ill-will and dissension, when one man arro-
gantly gives the preference to this saint and one man
to another. If you want to know things like that and
spend time looking for the answers, you get no profit
from it, and it displeases the saints. *God is the author
of peace, not of disorder,*[3] and this peace consists of
true humility, not exaltation of self.

Some people are drawn strongly towards one saint or
another by the very warmth of their affection, but it is
a human emotion, not a God-inspired one. I am the
foundation of all the saints—I gave them grace and
granted them glory. I know the merits of each one—I
went before them with the blessings of my sweetness;
I knew my beloved from the first before all ages. I
singled them out from the world[4]—they did not first
choose me. I called them by my grace, I drew them
by my mercy. I led them through all kinds of temptations, I poured out wondrous comfort on them. I gave
them perseverance, I rewarded their patience. I know
the greatest and the least, I embrace them all with a
love that cannot be told. I am to be praised for all my
saints, blessed and honoured above all for everyone, for
it was I that chose them out and made them great and
glorious, when they had no merit of their own. Anyone
who fails to honour one of the least of my saints fails
to honour the great, for I *made great and little alike.*[5]
Anyone who disparages any one of the saints disparages
me and all others in the kingdom of heaven. They are
all one, bound together by love. Their thoughts and
their wills are one, and mutual love unites them; and
what is nobler still, they love me more than themselves
and their own merits. They are rapt outside themselves,
raised beyond the love of self; they pass altogether into
love for me, and there they rest in joy. Nothing can
turn them away or cast them down from there, for

³ I Cor. 14.33   ⁴ John 15.19   ⁵ Wisdom 6.8

they are filled with the eternal truth, and burn with the flame of inextinguishable love.

So people who are still worldly and unregenerate must argue no more about the standing of the saints, for the only love they know is one that serves their personal pleasure. Such people add or take away according to their own inclinations, not in accordance with the eternal truth. There is much ignorance, particularly in those who have received little enlightenment and who rarely learn how to love anyone with a perfect spiritual love. They are drawn to this person or that by natural affection or human friendship, and they imagine that heavenly beings live in the same state as they do here below. But there is a world of difference between the thoughts of imperfect men and the insight given by revelation from above to men who are spiritually enlightened.

So, my son, you must beware of curiosity and meddling with things beyond your understanding. Instead, make it your business and concern to be found in the kingdom of heaven yourself, even if you are the least significant there. Even if a man knew which saint was more holy than another, or who was considered greatest in the kingdom of heaven, this knowledge would do him no good unless it made him humble himself before me and rise up to praise my name still more. God is pleased with a man who thinks about the greatness of his own sins and the poverty of his own virtues and how far off he is from the perfection of the saints, rather than with a man who debates which of the saints is more or less important. It is better to entreat the saints with prayers and tears of devotion, and humbly ask for their glorious intercession, than to indulge in empty curiosity and try to search out their secrets.

The saints are well content if men know how to be contented and to check their foolish speaking. They do not glory in any merit of their own, for they do not credit themselves with any goodness but ascribe it all to me, since I gave them all out of my boundless love. They are so filled with love of God and with over-flowing joy that their glory is complete and nothing could increase their happiness. The higher the saints are in glory, the humbler they are in their own sight, and the closer and the dearer they are to me. This is why you find it written: They fell down in worship before him who lives for ever and ever, and threw down their crowns before God, and fell on their faces before the Lamb.[6]

Many people ask who is the greatest in the kingdom of God, when they do not know whether they themselves will be fit to be reckoned among the least. It is a great thing to be even the least in heaven where everyone is great, because they will all be the sons of God, and that will be their name. *The meanest of them shall be ancestor to a thousand,*[7] *and young he dies that dies a hundred years old.*[8]

When the disciples asked who was greatest in the kingdom of heaven, this is the reply they received: *Unless you become like little children again, you shall not enter the kingdom of heaven. He is greatest in the kingdom of heaven who will abase himself like this little child.*[9] Woe upon those who are too proud to humble themselves with little children, for the humble door of the heavenly kingdom will not let them through. Woe upon those who are rich, they have their comfort already,[10] for when the poor are going into the kingdom of God, they will stand weeping outside. Rejoice, you who are humble; be glad, you who are poor, for *the kingdom of God is yours,*[11] if only you are following the way of truth.

---

[6] Apoc. 4.9-10   [7] Is. 60.22   [8] Is. 65.20
[9] Matt. 18.3-4   [10] Luke 6.24   [11] Luke 6.20

LIX

Hope and confidence must be fixed on God alone

THE DISCIPLE : O Lord God, whose mercies cannot be counted, you are my confidence in this life, and my greatest comfort of all that exists below the sky. When did things ever go well for me without you? When could they ever go ill when you were there? I would rather be in poverty for your sake, than be rich and lose your presence. I would rather wander this earth and have you near me, than possess heaven itself without you. Where you are, there heaven is too; where you are not is death and hell. You are all I long for, and so I must needs reach out to you with tears and cries and prayers. There is no one but you, my God, on whom I can rely to stand beside me and help me in my need; you are my hope and my confidence, my comforter, faithful in all things.

One and all have their own interest at heart,[1] but you intend nothing but my salvation and my progress, and make everything contribute to my good. You may expose me to all kinds of temptations and misfortunes, but it is all planned for my benefit, for you always test those you love in all kinds of ways. When you test me like this, you are worthy of love and praise no less than if you were filling me with heavenly comfort. Wherever I look outside you there is weakness and inconstancy; and so, O God, my Lord, in you I find my only hope and refuge, and with you I leave my troubles and my sorrows.

Crowds of friends will be of no use, and strong supporters will have no power to help; wise counsellors will not give good advice, and learned books will bring no

[1] Phil. 2.21

comfort; no precious substance will liberate, no lovely hidden spot protect, unless you draw near, help, comfort and console me, teach me and keep me safe. For all the things that seem to contribute to our peace and blessedness are ineffective and can bring no happiness without you. You are the goal of all that is good, you are true sublimity of life, true depth of wisdom; and your servants find their most lasting comfort if beyond all things they rest their hopes in you. I look to you; I trust in you, my God and merciful Father.

Bless my soul and sanctify it with the blessing of heaven, so that it may become your holy house, the seat of your eternal glory. In this temple where your greatness rests, let nothing be found which can offend your eyes, O God of majesty.

Look down upon me in the wealth of your goodness, in the abundance of your pity.[2] Hear the prayer of your poor servant, a far-off exile in a land where death overshadows him.[3] Protect and preserve the soul of your helpless servant amidst the dangers of this mortal life; send grace to accompany him and guide him by the path of peace to the land of never-fading glory. Amen.

---

[2] Ps. 50.2; Ps. 68.17   [3] Is. 9.2

BOOK 4

A REVERENT RECOMMENDATION TO HOLY COMMUNION

THE VOICE OF CHRIST

Come to me, all you that labour and are burdened; I will give you rest.

This bread which I am to give is my flesh, given for the life of the world.

Take, eat; this is my body, given up for you. Do this for a commemoration of me.

He who eats my flesh and drinks my blood lives continually in me, and I in him.

The words I have been speaking to you are spirit and life.

I

Christ must be received with great reverence

THE VOICE OF THE DISCIPLE: O Christ, the eternal Truth, these are your words, though they were not spoken all at one time or recorded all in one place. They are your words, and they are true, and so I must accept them with gratitude and faith. They are yours, you spoke them. They are mine as well, because you proclaimed them for my salvation. I receive them gladly from your lips, so that they may be firmly grafted in my heart. Such loving words, so full of sweetness and affection, they draw me to you—but my own sins frighten me away. When I think of receiving so great a mystery, the knowledge of my guilt repels me. Your sweet words invite me, but the weight of my sins holds me back.

You bid me come to you with confidence, if I wish to have any companionship with you. You bid me take the food of immortality, if I desire to attain eternal life and glory. *Come to me,* you say, *all you that labour and are burdened; I will give you rest.*[1] How sweet and kind that sounds to a sinner; for you, O Lord my God, are here inviting one who is destitute and worthless to share your most holy body.

But who am I, Lord, to presume to approach you? The very heavens cannot contain you,[2] and yet you say, *Come to me, all of you?* What does it mean, this affection and kindness, this loving invitation? How dare I come, when I know there is no goodness in me to give me a right to come? How can I bring you into my house, when I have so often offended your kindly eyes? The angels and archangels feel awe before you, the saints and the upright fear—and yet you say, *Come to me, all of you?* If anyone said this but you, Lord, who would believe it was true? If anyone called us but you, Lord, who would dare to draw near?

Noah was a good man, and he worked for a hundred years to build the ark, so that he and a few others might be saved. How can I in one hour prepare myself to receive with reverence him who built the world?

Moses your servant was a great man and your especial friend. He built an ark of wood that would not rot, and covered it with purest gold, so that he could put in it the tablets on which the law was written. Shall I, a creature subject to decay, find it so easy to receive you, the author of that law, the giver of all life?

Solomon, the wisest of the kings of Israel, was seven years building a splendid temple to bring honour to your name, and the festival of its dedication he cele-

[1] Matt. 11.28   [2] III Kings 8.27

brated for eight whole days. He offered a thousand peace-offerings, and laid the ark of the covenant in the place prepared for it with all solemnity and rejoicing and the sound of trumpets. How can I bring you into my house, when I am such a poor creature, the most worthless of men, who hardly know how to spend half an hour in devotion? Why, I find myself wishing I had even once spent half an hour as I ought!

How eager they were to please you, O my God! How feeble is the little that I do, how short the time I spend on preparing myself to communicate! Rarely do I gather my thoughts together, very rarely am I free from all distraction. Yet in the healing presence of the very Deity, surely no unfitting thought should cross my mind, no created thing should occupy my thinking. It is no angel, but the Lord of angels that I am to receive as my guest.

Yet there is a great difference between the ark of the covenant and the relics it held, and your most pure body with its inexpressible virtues; between those sacrifices that the law established to foreshadow what was yet to come, and the true offering of your body, bringing to fulfilment all the sacrifices of old. Why then do I not prepare with more concern to receive your holy gifts, seeing that those saints of old, the patriarchs and prophets, the kings and princes with all their peoples, showed such feeling and devotion when they worshipped God?

David, that devout king, went dancing with all his might[3] before the ark of the Lord as he recalled the blessings God gave to his ancestors. He made musical instruments and composed songs of praise; he taught the people to sing with joy, and himself played upon the harp as the Holy Spirit breathed upon him. He

[3] II Kings 6.14

taught the people of Israel to praise God with all their hearts, and daily to bless him and proclaim his name with sweet-sounding voices.

If they felt such devotion and were so moved to praise God when they saw the ark of the covenant, how much reverence and devotion ought to be felt by me and every Christian person in the presence of the Sacrament, in receiving the most excellent body of Christ!

Many people go running off to various places to see the relics of the saints; they hear about the miracles they did, and gaze in wonder at the great churches built over them. They feast their eyes on their holy bones wrapped up in silk and gold, and press their lips to them. Yet here before my eyes on the altar, you, my God, are present yourself, holier than all the saints, creator of men and Lord of angels.

It is curiosity and the love of novelty that takes men to see such things, but they return with little harvest in the way of improved lives, especially when they embark on such visits thoughtlessly and with no real sorrow for sin. But here in the sacrament of the altar you are wholly present, my God, the man Christ Jesus; and whenever you are received worthily and with real devotion, there the rich harvest of eternal salvation is brought in. Men are not drawn there by thoughtlessness or curiosity, or the desire to gratify the senses, but by firm faith, reverent hope and sincere love.

O unseen God, establisher of the world, how wonderfully you deal with us; how gentle and how gracious is your design for those you have chosen, when in the Sacrament you set your very self before them that they may take you! This thought surpasses all understanding; this above all draws the devout and kindles love in their hearts. For those who really trust in you and lay open their whole lives to be put right, through this most worthy Sacrament receive the grace of devotion and the love of goodness.

How wonderful is the hidden grace of the Sacrament! Only those who trust Christ know it, while those who are faithless and slaves to sin can have no knowledge of it. In this Sacrament grace is granted to the spirit, lost virtue restored to the soul, and beauty renewed that was marred by sin. This grace is sometimes so great and brings such richness of devotion, that not only the mind but the weak body too is conscious of power imparted to it.

In Christ lies all the hope and merit of those who shall be saved, and yet we do not feel a stronger love impelling us to partake of him. What sorrow and grief we should feel at our coldness and lack of concern! For he is our sanctification and our atonement;[4] he is the comfort of the traveller and the eternal joy of the saint.

It is a sad thing that so many people pay so little attention to this saving mystery, which fills heaven with joy and brings this whole world health.

How hard and blind the heart of man must be to give so little thought to this unspeakable gift, and even to drift into indifference through seeing it every day! If this most holy Sacrament were celebrated in one place only in the whole world, what a longing would draw men to that place and to such a priest of God, so that they too might see the divine mystery performed! But as it is, many have been made priests, and Christ is offered up in many places, and by the diffusion of this holy communion throughout the whole world, God's grace and love to man is more fully revealed.

Good Jesus, eternal shepherd, we bring our thanks to you, because with your precious body and blood you

4 I Cor. 1.30

graciously restore us in our poverty and exile, and with your own lips you invite us to share this mystery, saying, *Come to me, all you that labour and are burdened; I will give you rest.*

II

The Sacrament reveals God's great goodness and love towards man

THE DISCIPLE : Trusting in your goodness and great mercy, Lord, I come—sick I come to my Saviour, hungry and thirsty to the well of life, needy to the King of Heaven, a servant to my Master, a creature to my Maker, distressed to him who loves and comforts me.

But how can it happen that you should come to me? Who am I, that you offer me yourself? How can a sinner dare to enter your presence? How can you stoop to come to a sinner? You know your servant—you know there is no good in him that you should give him this.

So I confess my worthlessness, but your goodness I acknowledge, your mercy I praise, and my thanks I offer for your great love. It is for your own sake that you do this, not because I deserve it. You want me to know your goodness; you want to grant me love and commend humility. Since you are content with this, since you have commanded that it should be so, I too am content that you should honour me. If only my wickedness did not stand in your way!

O Jesus, most sweet and kind, what reverence and gratitude and never-ceasing praise we owe for the privilege of receiving your holy body, whose worth no man living can express. What thoughts shall fill my mind in this communion, as I draw near to my God? I cannot worship him as I ought, and yet I long to receive him with devotion. The best and most profitable thing I can do is to humble myself utterly before you, and exalt your infinite goodness above me. I praise you, my God, and exalt you for ever. Myself I despise, and I submit to your will in the abyss of my worthlessness.

See, you are unutterably holy—I am the foulest of sinners. Yet how amazing—you stoop down to me when I am not fit to raise my eyes to you. To think that you come to me, you desire my company, you invite me to your feast! You want to give me the bread of heaven, the food of angels to eat,[1] your very self, the living bread, that has *come down from heaven, and gives life to the whole world.*[2]

See the love streaming out, see what graciousness is shining there! What thanks and praise we owe you in return! What thought for our health and well-being you showed when you instituted this! How sweet and lovely you made the feast when you gave yourself for food! How wonderful, O Lord, are your acts, how strong your might, how infallible your truth! You gave the word and everything was made; and this is done which you commanded. It is a wonderful thing, deserving faith, a thing beyond all human understanding, that you, O Lord my God, true God and man, are wholly contained in the form of a little bread and wine, and are eaten by those who receive you, yet are not consumed.

Lord of all, who have no need of anyone, it was your choice to live within us by this Sacrament of yours. Preserve my heart and body without stain, that with a glad clear conscience I may be enabled to celebrate this

[1] Ps. 77.25   [2] John 6.33

mystery often, and to receive to my salvation this rite that you have authorized and established, to bring you especial honour and to be a perpetual memorial feast.

My soul, rejoice and offer thanks to God for this noble gift, this wonderful source of consolation left in this vale of tears for you. Whenever you repeat this mystery and receive the body of Christ, you perform the work of your redemption and become a sharer in all the merits of Christ. For the love of Christ is never diminished, his great atonement can never be used up.

You should therefore always prepare yourself for this by a renewal of your mind,[3] and think most carefully about this great mystery that brings salvation. Whenever you celebrate or hear the Mass it should seem as new, as wonderful, and as joyful to you, as if on this very day Christ first came down to the Virgin's womb and was made man, or first hung on the cross, and suffered and died for man's salvation.

III

It is a help to communicate often

THE DISCIPLE : See, Lord, it is I that come to you, so that I may be blessed with your gift and made glad at the sacred banquet, where you have made bounteous provision, O God, for your pensioners.[1] You are my salvation and my redemption, my hope and strength, my beauty and my glory—all that I can or should desire is to be found in you.

Comfort your servant's heart then on this day, this heart that aspires, Lord Jesus, to you.[2] I desire to receive you now with reverence and devotion; I long to bring you to my house, so that I may receive a blessing

[3] Eph. 4.23   [1] Ps. 67.11   [2] Ps. 85.4

with Zacchaeus and be counted among the sons of Abraham.[3] My soul is filled with yearning for your body, my heart longs to be one with you. Give yourself to me, and I shall be content, for nothing other than you can really comfort me.

I cannot exist without you; without your presence I have no strength to live. Therefore I must come to you often and receive you for my healing and my salvation, else I shall grow faint on my journey if I miss my heavenly food; just as you once said, most merciful Jesus, when you were preaching to the people and healing diseases of every sort,[4] *I must not send them away fasting, or perhaps they will grow faint on their journey.*[5] Feed me now as you did those people then, seeing that you have left yourself in the Sacrament to comfort those who trust you. You are the sweet refreshment of the soul, and the man who takes you as he should shall inherit a share in the eternal glory.

I so often fall and do wrong, I so soon cease to care and give up; and so I must often pray and make my confession and receive your holy body, so that I may be cleansed, renewed and inspired again. If I keep away too long, I shall drift from my holy purpose. Man *has all the thoughts of his heart, even in youth, so bent towards evil,*[6] and unless God's cure is applied, he quickly goes from bad to worse. And so the Holy Communion serves to pluck a man back from evil and confirm him in what is good. If I am so often thoughtless and unmoved now when I am communicating or celebrating, what would happen if I did not apply this remedy, or seek out such a great help? Though I am not fit and in a proper frame of mind to celebrate every day, yet I will take care to receive the divine mysteries at suitable times, and to present myself to receive a share of such great grace. For as long as the faithful

[3] Luke 19.9   [4] Mark 1.34
[5] Matt. 15.32   [6] Gen. 8.21

soul is exiled from your presence in this mortal body,[7] its one chief consolation is to think often of its God, and to receive its Beloved with a heart full of devotion.

How wonderful is the meekness of your love to us! —for you, O Lord God, the creator and giver of life to every spirit, humble yourself enough to come to the poverty-stricken soul, and in your full Godhead and humanity you pour out your riches to satisfy its hungry need. How happy the mind and how blessed the soul, that is found worthy to receive her Lord and God with devotion, and in receiving him, be filled with spiritual joy! How great the Lord that she receives, how lovely the guest that she invites; how delightful a companion, how faithful a friend she finds; how fair and noble a bridegroom she embraces, one to be loved beyond all that is dear and all that can be desired.

My sweet beloved, before your face may heaven and earth and all that makes them fair keep silent. All their praise and their loveliness are gifts from your generous hand, and they cannot compare with the loveliness of the name of God, whose wisdom is inscrutable.[8]

IV

Many good things are imparted through the Communion to those who approach it devoutly

THE DISCIPLE: O Lord my God, come to meet your servant with the blessings of your sweetness, so that I may be enabled to draw near devoutly and as I ought to your wonderful Sacrament.

Stir up my heart with love for you, strip off the indifference that numbs me. Come and strengthen me with

[7] II Cor. 5.6   [8] Ps. 146.5

your aid,[1] so that my spirit may drink in your sweetness, concealed beneath this Sacrament in a welling
spring. Give light to my eyes so that I may see this
great mystery. Strengthen me with undoubting faith to
believe it. For here you are at work—it is no human
power. It is your holy institution, and no contrivance
of man. No man of himself is capable of grasping and
understanding these things which are beyond even the
subtlety of angels. I am an unworthy sinner, nothing
but dust and ashes—how can I look into this deep
secret and understand it? Lord, I come to you with all
the sincerity of my heart, and with good firm faith; I
come with hope and reverence, because you have commanded it, and I really believe that you are present
here in the Sacrament, both God and man.

It is your wish that I should receive you and become
one with you in love. I therefore pray you for your
mercy, and beg you to grant me special grace, so that
I may melt away in love and be absorbed in you, no
more concerned for any outside comfort. For this
Sacrament is most high and most worthy. It is the
health of soul and body, the remedy for every sickness
of the spirit. By it my faults are cured, my passions
curbed, temptations overcome or weakened. Grace is
outpoured in richer measure, virtue that has taken root
is strengthened; faith is increased, hope made strong,
love kindled to envelop all my being.

O God, as those you love communicate devoutly, you
have used the Sacrament to pour out on them abundant blessings, and you do so still, O comforter of the
soul, O help of human weakness, O giver of every
inward joy. For on your beloved you bestow abundant comfort to help them in every kind of trouble; you
raise them from the depths of their despair to trust in
your protection, and in their hearts you refresh and

[1] Ps. 105.4

enlighten them by some new grace. And so those who before Communion felt ill at ease and empty of affection find themselves refreshed by the heavenly food and drink and changed to a better state.

You deal with your chosen ones like this in wisdom, so that they may truly and unmistakably recognize how weak they are of themselves, and how far they depend on you for grace and goodness. Of themselves, they are cold, hard, and empty of devotion, but through you they become fervent, eager, devout.

Who can come in humility to the well of sweetness without carrying away even a little sweetness with him? Who can stand near the blazing fire without absorbing a little warmth? You are the well that is always full and always overflowing, the fire that burns continually, never dying down. So even if I cannot draw from the reservoir itself, even if I cannot drink my fill, yet I will put my mouth to a crack in the heavenly pipe and get at least a tiny drip to moisten my dry lips and keep me from withering away. Even if I am as yet unable to be heavenly through and through, all aflame like the Cherubim and Seraphim, yet I will try to strive towards devotion and to prepare my heart, so that by humbly receiving the life-giving Sacrament I may achieve even a flicker of the flame of God.

Whatever I lack, good Jesus, most holy Saviour, do you provide for me in your graciousness and kindness; for you were ready to call us all to yourself, when you said, *Come to me, all you that labour and are burdened; I will give you rest.* I certainly labour with the sweat of my brow,[2] the sorrows of my heart bring me grief; I am burdened with sins, I am harassed by temptations; all kinds of evil emotions enmesh me and hold me down. There is no one to help me, no one to set me free and save me, but you my Lord, my God, my Saviour. To you I commit myself and all I have, that

[2] Gen. 3.19

you may watch over me and guide me to eternal life. Receive me, and so your name shall be praised and glorified, seeing that you have set out your body and blood to be my food and drink. O Lord God, my Saviour, grant that as this mystery is repeated, so my love and devotion may grow.

V

The dignity of the Sacrament and the position of the priest

THE VOICE OF THE BELOVED : If you had the purity of angels and the holiness of St John the Baptist, you would not be fit to receive or handle this Sacrament. It is not due to any merit on the part of man, that a man should consecrate and handle the Sacrament of Christ and take for his food the bread of angels. It is an exalted ministry that the priest fulfils and his rank is high, for to him is given a thing which is not granted to angels; for only priests, duly ordained in the Church, have the power to celebrate and consecrate the body of Christ.

Now a priest is the minister of God, using the word of God by God's command and institution, but it is God who is the chief author there; he is the unseen operator in control of everything that he wills, obeyed by everything that he commands. In this most excellent Sacrament therefore you should put your trust in God the all-powerful, not in your own feelings or in any outward sign. So it is with awe and reverence that you should approach this work.

Consider yourself, and think what kind of ministry has been entrusted to you by the laying on of the bishop's hands. You have actually been made a priest, and consecrated to celebrate. See then that you offer sacrifice to God in due time with faith and devotion, and show yourself blameless. You have not made your task lighter, but now you are bound with a tighter bond of discipline, and greater perfection in holiness is required of you. A priest must be clothed with all the virtues and must show to others the example of a good life. His manner of life is not that of the ordinary and common ways of men, but is shared with the angels or perfect men on earth.

When the priest is wearing the holy vestments he stands in the place of Christ so that he may humbly and prayerfully entreat God both for himself and for all the people. Before and behind he bears the sign of the Lord's cross so that he may continually remember the Passion of Christ. Before him he bears the cross on the chasuble, so that he may carefully mark the footsteps of Christ and make it his fervent desire to follow in them. On his back he is signed with the cross so that he may for God's sake endure with mildness any adversity that others bring upon him. He bears the cross before him so that he may mourn his own sins; he bears it behind him so that he may in compassion grieve for others' sins as well; and so that he may realize that he has been set in the midst between God and the sinner, and never grow weary of prayer and the holy oblation until his prayer for grace and mercy wins an answer.

When the priest celebrates, he is honouring God. To the angels he brings joy, and the Church he strengthens; the living he helps, and for the departed he obtains rest. Himself he makes a sharer in all good things.

VI

The disciple asks how to prepare for Communion

O Lord, when I consider your excellence and my own worthlessness, I am very much afraid and stand in utter dismay. If I do not approach, I am running away from life; and if I present myself in an unfit state, I incur your displeasure. O God, you are my helper and my counsellor in need—what am I to do?

Teach me the right way. Set before me some brief exercise suitable for Holy Communion. I need to know how to prepare my heart for you in devotion and reverence, if I am to receive your Sacrament to my salvation, or if I am to celebrate a sacrifice so great and so divine.

VII

Examine your conscience and resolve to amend

THE VOICE OF THE BELOVED : Above all else, when God's priest is going to celebrate the Sacrament, to handle and receive it, he must approach with great humility in his heart and with lowly reverence. He must come in full faith, with the loving intention of honouring God.

Look very carefully into your own conscience, and clean and purify it to the best of your ability by true repentance and humble confession. Then you will have nothing on your mind, no awareness of guilt that will disquiet you and prevent you from approaching freely. You must feel disgust at all your sins in general, and sorrow and pain in particular for the things you do wrong every day. If you have time, confess to God in the secrecy of your own heart the wretched state of all your emotions.

You must feel sorry and bewail the fact that you are still so unspiritual and worldly, still so much alive to all your personal desires; so full of turbulent longings, so unguarded where your senses are concerned;

so often wrapped up in foolish imaginings;

so attracted to outward things, so remiss about the life within;

so easily induced to laugh and slacken control, so hardened against tears and compunction;

so ready for ease and physical comfort, so reluctant to accept hardship with enthusiasm;

so eager to hear news and see pleasant things, so slow to embrace what is lowly and poor;

so greedy for possessions, so mean in giving, so grasping to keep what you have;

so thoughtless when you speak, so talkative when silence should be observed;

so unsettled in your habits, so impatient in all you do;

so enthusiastic over food, so deaf to the word of God;

so quick to rest, so slow to toil;

so wide-awake to listen to gossip, so sleepy at the sacred vigils;

so eager to get to the end, so wandering in attention;

so perfunctory in reciting the hours, so cold in cele-brating, so unmoved in communicating;

so easily distracted, so rarely concentrated;

so quickly moved to anger, so apt to take offence at others;

so ready to judge, so harsh in finding fault;

so happy in prosperity, so feeble when things go wrong;

so full of good intentions, and achieving such poor results.

When you have confessed and wept over these and

all your other failings with sorrow and real dissatisfaction at your weakness, set up a firm resolve to be always improving your life, and to make better progress.

Then in complete surrender, wholeheartedly offer up yourself to the honour of my name as a perpetual burnt offering on the altar of your heart, committing your body and soul in faith to me. So you will be enabled to come worthily to offer sacrifice to God, and to take the Sacrament of my body to your salvation.

The most worthy offering and the greatest reparation to wipe out sins is the offering of oneself wholly and entirely to God together with the offering of the body of Christ in the Mass and in the Communion. If a man does all that he can and feels true repentance whenever he comes to me for mercy and for grace, *as I am a living God,* says the Lord, *the sinner's death is none of my contriving! I would have him leave his sinning and live on.*[1] *For his transgressions shall be forgotten,*[2] and he shall be forgiven them all.

VIII

Christ's offering on the cross and our surrender of ourselves

THE VOICE OF THE BELOVED : I freely surrendered myself to God the Father for your sins, with my hands spread out on the cross and my body stripped. I kept nothing back, but let all be transformed into a sacrifice to appease the divine anger. And every day in the Mass, you too should of your own free will offer your-

[1] Ezech. 33.11   [2] Ezech. 18.22

self to me as a pure and holy offering with all your powers and affections, from the very depths of your heart.

I ask nothing more of you except that you should want to surrender yourself entirely to me. I do not care what you give me besides yourself, because I do not want your gifts, but you. If you possessed everything except me, you would not find satisfaction. In the same way, nothing you give me can please me if you do not give yourself. Give yourself to me. Offer yourself wholly for God's sake, and your offering will be accepted. Think of this—I offered myself wholly to the Father for your sake. I even gave my whole body and my blood to feed you, so that I should be entirely yours, and you should be kept mine. If you hold to yourself and do not willingly surrender yourself to my will, there is something missing from your offering and the union between us cannot be complete.

If you want to achieve liberty and grace, the willing surrender of yourself into the hands of God is more important than all your works. The reason why so few people become spiritually enlightened and free within is because they do not know how to give up all claim to themselves. What I said is still unchanged: *None of you can be my disciple if he does not take leave of all that he possesses.*[1] So if you want to be my disciple, give yourself to me with all your powers of feeling.

[1] Luke 14.33

IX

We must offer to God ourselves and all that we have, and pray for all people

THE VOICE OF THE DISCIPLE : O Lord, everything in heaven and on this earth is yours. It is my desire to bring you myself as a free-will offering and to remain yours for ever. O Lord, with sincerity in my heart I offer you myself today to be your servant always, to obey you and to offer you continually the sacrifice of praise. Receive me together with the holy offering of your precious body, which I make to you today in the unseen presence of angels who assist me. May it bring health to me and to all your people.

O Lord, I bring you all my sins and all the wrong things I have done in your sight and in the sight of your holy angels, from the very first day I was capable of sinning, right up to this present time. I offer them on your altar of atonement so that you may burn them all together, consume them in the flame of your love, wipe out all the stains of my sins and cleanse my conscience from every wrong. Renew to me the gift of your grace which I lost by sinning; grant me in abundance all I need, and in your mercy receive me and give me the kiss of peace.

What can I do for my sins except confess them humbly, grieve for them, and pray you without ceasing for propitiation? I do pray to you—hear me, O God, in mercy, as I stand before you. The thought of all my sins is hateful to me, and I never want to commit them again. I am sorry for them, and shall be sorry as long as I live. I am ready to do penance and make amends to the best of my ability. Forgive me, O God, forgive me my sins for the sake of your holy name. Save this soul of mine which you redeemed with your precious blood. Here I am; I commit myself to your mercy, and resign myself into your hands. Deal with me as your goodness prompts, not as my wickedness and sinful ways deserve.

I also bring you all I have that is good, though it is imperfect and there is little of it. I pray you to improve it and sanctify it, to look favourably on it and make it fit to receive; and to draw it always nearer to perfection. And lead me also, slow, useless and pitiful as I am, to a good and blessed end.

I also bring you all the holy desires of those who love you, the needs of parents, friends, brothers, sisters, of all I hold dear, and of all who for love of you have done some kindness to myself or others, and who have asked me to say prayers and masses for themselves and all they love, whether they are still alive and in the body, or whether they have gone from this world. May they all know the help of your grace, the aid of your comfort, protection from danger and release from punishment; may they be delivered from every evil and praise you with joy and thanksgiving.

I also bring you prayers and the atoning sacrifice especially for those who have harmed me in some way, who have made me unhappy or abused me, caused me some loss or inflicted some burden; also for those whom I have made unhappy at any time, whom I have distressed, burdened or shocked by word or deed, knowingly or unknowingly. Forgive us all equally for our sins and the wrongs we have done each other. Take away from our hearts, Lord, all suspicion, resentment, anger, and quarrelling, anything that can do love some hurt and lessen brotherly affection.

Take pity, O Lord, take pity on those who seek your mercy, give grace to those who need it. Grant that we may so live that we may be found worthy to know your grace and attain eternal life. Amen.

X

The Communion must not be lightly abandoned

THE VOICE OF THE BELOVED : If you are to be healed of your passions and faults, if you are to find strength and vigilance in the face of all the temptations and wiles of the Devil, you must return time and time again to the spring of grace and divine mercy, to the well-head of goodness and all purity.

Your enemy knows that the most effective remedy and the greatest spiritual profit lie in the Communion, so he tries as hard as he can in every way to draw the faithful and devout away, and to keep them from it. It is when they set about preparing themselves for the Holy Communion that some people suffer the worst attacks of Satan. For the Wicked Spirit himself, as it says in the Book of Job, comes among the sons of God,[1] so that he can upset them with his practised villainy, and make them fearful or perplexed; he hopes in this way to weaken their desire or attack their faith and destroy it, so that they will either abandon Communion altogether or come halfheartedly.

But you must not pay any attention to his tricks and suggestions, however foul and frightening they may be, but hurl all such visions back on his own head. You

[1] Job 1.6-7

must scorn the wretch and laugh at him. Holy Communion must not be neglected for any assaults and commotions of his.

People are often hindered by being too anxious to feel devotion, and by worrying about their confession. Follow the advice of the wise, and lay aside worry and doubt, because they are a hindrance to the grace of God and destroy the spirit of devotion.

Do not put off the Holy Communion because of some little trouble or weight on your mind, but go quickly to confession, and freely forgive others for all they have done to offend you. If you have offended anyone else, humbly pray for mercy and God will readily forgive you.

What good does it do to put off your confession and let the Communion wait? Get yourself cleansed as soon as possible, spit out the poison at once; come quickly for the remedy, and it will do you more good than if you make it wait. If you put it off today for one thing, something worse will probably happen tomorrow; and so you might be kept from the Communion for a long time, and become all the time less fit for it. Shake off this heaviness and irresolution as soon as you possibly can. There is no point in tormenting yourself, and being ill at ease, and keeping yourself away from the divine institution, because of obstacles that arise afresh every day. It does more harm to postpone the Communion, because doing so often makes a man spiritually lazy.

It is a shameful fact that some halfhearted and undisciplined people are glad to find some excuse for putting off their confession, and they want to postpone the Holy Communion for fear they might be obliged to pay more attention to self-discipline. How feeble their love and how weak their devotion must be when they find it so easy to let the Communion wait!

On the other hand, a man is happy himself and pleasing to God, if he keeps his conscience unstained and lives in such a way that he is prepared and ready to communicate every day if he is permitted, and if he can do so without causing others to comment.

If a man keeps away sometimes out of humility or for some legitimate cause, he deserves praise for his reverent attitude; but if it is laziness that has crept up on him, he must exert himself and shake himself free. Then the Lord will strengthen his desire because of his good intention, for he considers that particularly. When a man is genuinely prevented, he will always have a good intention and a holy desire to communicate, and so he will not be deprived of the fruit of the Sacrament. For anyone who knows devotion can freely have spiritual communion with Christ every day and at every moment to his own great profit; for he shares a mystic communion and is invisibly refreshed whenever he devoutly meditates on the mystery of Christ's incarnation and his passion, and is filled with a burning love for him. (Yet on certain days and at proper times he should with love and reverence receive the body of his Redeemer sacramentally—but seeking rather to praise and honour God than find comfort for himself.)

A man who only prepares because a festival is approaching or because he has to conform to custom will often be unprepared.

If a man offers himself to God as a whole burnt-offering whenever he celebrates or communicates, then he is really blessed.

When you are celebrating, do not be too slow or too quick, but observe some good practice in common with those with whom you live. You should not cause others irritation or annoyance, but observe some way in common as appointed by men of more authority, and consider the good of others, rather than your own feelings and your own devotion.

XI

The body of Christ and the Holy Scriptures are essential to the faithful soul

THE VOICE OF THE DISCIPLE : Sweetest Lord Jesus, what delight fills the devout soul as it feasts with you at your banquet! There no other food is set before it but you, its sole beloved, desirable beyond all that heart can long for. What a wonderful thing it would be if I had such love in my heart that I could weep in your presence, if I could wash your feet with tears as the Magdalene did in love.[1] But where is this love, where is this flood of holy tears? As I stand before you and before your holy angels, my whole heart should be burning and weeping tears of joy, since you are really present to me in the Sacrament. It is true that you are hidden under a different form, but my eyes could not bear to look at you in the full brightness of your divinity. Not even the world itself could survive amidst the lightnings of your majesty and glory; and so when you conceal yourself beneath the Sacrament, it is my weakness you consider. Yet I really have and adore the one whom angels adore in heaven. I only see him meanwhile by faith, but they see him as he is with no veil between.

I must content myself with the light of true faith and guide my steps by it, until the day of eternal brightness breaks over me and all shadowy symbols retire.[2] When the time of fulfilment comes[3] the use of sacraments will cease, for the blessed ones in the glory of heaven have no need of the sacramental remedy.

[1] Luke 7.38   [2] Cant. 2.16-17   [3] I Cor. 13.10

They rejoice endlessly in the presence of God, seeing his glory face to face,[4] and are transfigured as they borrow glory from the glory of the immeasurable Godhead,[5] and taste the word of God made flesh, who was from the first and lasts for ever.[6]

When I think of all these wonderful things, even spiritual comfort becomes distasteful to me, because as long as I am not seeing my Lord openly and in his glory, I can find no value in anything I see or hear in this world. O God, you know it is true that nothing can comfort me, that no created thing can satisfy my longing, but only you, my God, whom I yearn to gaze on for ever. But that is impossible as long as I remain in this mortal body; so I must be prepared to exercise patience, and with all my desiring, to submit myself to you. While they were alive, the saints who now rejoice with you in the kingdom of heaven had to wait in faith and patience for the dawning of your glory. What they believed, I believe; the hopes they held, I hold; and through your grace I trust that I shall reach the place where they have gone. Meanwhile, I will guide my steps by faith, and draw strength from the example of the saints. I also have my holy books to comfort me and to show me how to live, and above all I have your most holy body to be my only refuge and my cure.

There are two things I find essential in this life, and without them this wretched existence would be unbearable. As long as I am detained in the prison of the body I need two things, and they are light and food. Therefore you have given your holy body to strengthen my weak mind and body, and you have given your word for a lamp to guide my feet.[7] Without these two things I cannot live as I ought, for the word of God is the

[4] I Cor. 13.12   [5] II Cor. 3.18
[6] John 1.14; I Peter 1.25; I John 1.1   [7] Ps. 118.105

light of my soul, and your Sacrament the bread that gives me life. They are like two tables, one on this side and one on that in the treasure-house of the holy Church. One table is the sacred altar with the holy bread, the precious body of Christ. The other is the Law of God containing the holy doctrine, which teaches us the true faith, and leads us unfalteringly to that inner sanctuary beyond the veil.[8]

Lord Jesus, light of the eternal light! I thank you for this table of sacred doctrine, which you have prepared for us through the prophets and apostles and other teachers who were your servants. O Creator and Redeemer of men, I thank you for your love for all the world, which you have declared by preparing this great banquet, where you set before us not the lamb of the Old Testament, but your own most holy body and blood. All the faithful you fill with joy at this sacred feast, making them merry with the cup of salvation, where all the delights of Paradise are found. And together with us the holy angels are feasting, though the delight they feel is a happier one than ours.

How great and honourable is the priest's office, for it is the priest who is allowed to use the sacred words and consecrate the Lord of majesty. It is the priest that blesses him with his lips, holds him in his hands, takes him with his mouth and ministers him to others.

How clean his hands must be! How pure his mouth, how holy his body, how free from stain his heart, seeing that the author of all purity so often enters him. From his lips must come nothing that is not holy, honourable and worth-while, seeing that he so often receives the Sacrament of Christ. His eyes must be sincere and modest, for they look on the body of Christ; his hands must be pure and raised to heaven, for they handle the Creator of heaven and earth. It is to the priest especi-

[8] Hebr. 9.3

ally that the command in the Law is addressed: *You must be men set apart, as I am set apart, I, the Lord your God.*[9]

God of all power, may your grace help us who have undertaken the duties of the priesthood, so that we may be able to serve you worthily and with devotion, with purity and a good conscience. If we are unable to live such blameless lives as we ought, grant that we may at least lament the wrong we have done, and serve you from now on with greater fervour, in the spirit of humility and determined to will aright.

XII

Before communicating you must prepare yourself very carefully for Christ

THE VOICE OF THE BELOVED: I am one that loves purity, and my gift is holiness. It is a pure heart that I seek, and there I take my rest. Prepare me a large upper room, furnished, and I will eat the paschal meal at your house with my disciples.[1] If you want me to come to you and stay with you, you must rid yourself of the leaven which remains over;[2] you must clean the house of your heart. Shut out all the world, and all the tumult of your sins; sit down by yourself like *a single sparrow on the house top,*[3] and think over your evil deeds in all the bitterness of your soul.

Any lover who is receiving her beloved prepares the best and finest place she can for him, for this is a sign of her love. But you must realize that you can never do enough by your own efforts to prepare yourself for your beloved, not even if you were to prepare for a

---

[9] Levit. 19.2
[2] I Cor. 5.7
[1] Mark 14.15; Luke 22.11-13
[3] Ps. 101.8

whole year and never think of anything else. It is only through my love and grace that you are allowed to come to my table at all; you are like a beggar invited to a rich man's dinner, who can do nothing to repay his kindness but humbly offer his thanks.

Do all you can, and do it as well as you can. Do not do it from habit, or because you must, but do it with awe and reverence, and receive the body of your beloved Lord with a response in your heart, as he stoops to come to you. It is I that called you; I commanded this to be done; I will supply your deficiencies. Come then, and take me.

When I give you the grace of devotion, thank your God for it, not because you have deserved it, but because I have taken pity on you. If on the other hand you find yourself unable to produce any emotion, give yourself to prayer; call out and beat on the door, and do not stop until you receive one little drop, one crumb of saving grace. You need me, but I do not need you. You do not come to sanctify me, but I come to sanctify you and make you a better person. You are coming to be sanctified by me and united to me, to receive fresh grace and inspiration that will help you to improve. Do not neglect this grace, but prepare your heart as carefully as you can, and bring into your house your beloved.

But it is not enough to prepare yourself to feel devotion before Communion; you must be careful to preserve yourself in that state after receiving the Sacrament. Watchfulness afterwards is demanded of you just as much as devout preparation beforehand; for watchfulness afterwards is the best way of preparing yourself for the gift of further grace, whereas a man loses all fitness for such a blessing if he immediately abandons himself to worldly comforts.

Beware of talking too much—keep in your secret place, and enjoy the presence of your God; in him you have the one person whom the whole world cannot take away. I am the one to whom you must wholly surrender yourself, so that from now on you may lose all your care and live not in yourself, but in me.

XIII

The devout soul should long wholeheartedly for union with Christ in the Sacrament

THE VOICE OF THE DISCIPLE : If only I could meet you, Lord, alone, and tell you the secrets of my heart; if only I could enjoy you as my soul desires, and *earn no contemptuous looks.*[1] If only there were no created thing to disturb me or give me a thought, but you and I could speak together alone, as two people who love each other speak, or as one friend delights to entertain another.

How I long and pray to separate my heart from all that is created and be wholly joined to you, and by means of the Holy Communion and frequent celebration to grow more and more to love the heavenly and eternal. O Lord God, when shall I be one with you, absorbed in you, with no more thought of self? You in me, and I in you—O make us one for ever. You are truly my sweetheart, known among ten thousand.[2] My soul is content to dwell in you all the days of its life. You are truly my peacemaker, my deepest peace and truest rest; away from you there is only toil and pain and endless wretchedness. Truly you are *a God of hidden ways;*[3] and your ways are not revealed to the ungodly, though you talk with the humble and simple.

O Lord, how sweet your spirit is ! You are ready to

[1] Cant. 8.1 [2] Cant. 5.10 [3] Is. 45.15

refresh your sons with that sweet bread that comes
down from heaven, in order to show them your kindness. *Indeed no other nation is so great; no other
nation has gods that draw near to it, as our God draws
near*[4] to all those who are faithful to him. For to them,
O God, you give yourself to eat and to enjoy, to comfort them day by day and raise their hearts to heaven.
What other nation can boast[5] as the people of Christ
can boast? Or is there any creature beneath the heaven
that is loved like the soul that is devout? God himself
comes to that soul and feeds it with his own glorious
body! What inexpressible grace, what unbelievable
mercy, what boundless love, poured out on man and on
no other!

What return shall I make to the Lord[6] for this grace,
for his wonderful love? I can do nothing that will
please him more than give him my whole heart, and
closely unite it to him. And then, when my soul is
perfectly joined to God, all that is within me will leap
up for joy. Then he will say to me, 'If you wish to be
with me, then it is my wish to be with you.' And I
shall reply to him, 'Lord, stay with me in your mercy.
I am very glad to be with you. The one thing that I
desire is for my heart to be one with you.'

XIV

On the burning desire which certain devout people feel for the body of Christ

THE DISCIPLE : *What treasures of loving-kindness, Lord,
dost thou store up for the men who fear thee.*[1]

When I think of certain devout people who approach
your Sacrament, Lord, with such great devotion and

4-5 Deut. 4.7-8   6 Ps. 115.3   1 Ps. 30.20

longing, I am often utterly ashamed. I blush to think
that I come so coldly and indifferently to your altar
and the table of Holy Communion, and that my heart
remains so unmoved and loveless. I feel no consuming
flame in your presence, O God; I am not drawn and
moved as many devout people have been, who could
not keep back their tears for their eager longing for
Communion, and the love that moved their hearts
Their bodies no less than their souls gasped, O God
for you, the living water; they could not satisfy or
appease their hunger except by receiving your body
with joy and spiritual longing. Their faith was a true
and burning faith, a reliable proof of your holy presence. For the people who really recognize their Lord
when the bread is broken are those whose hearts burn
within them as Jesus walks with them.[2] But such feeling
and devotion, such powerful love and longing, are often
far from me.

Good Jesus, who are so kind and gracious, be merciful to me. Grant that this needy, destitute creature may
sometimes in the Holy Communion feel even a little
love for you stirring in his heart. Grant that his faith
may be strengthened, his hope in your goodness increase, that love may be kindled and once it has tasted
the heavenly manna, may never fade away.

Your pity is able to grant even me this longed-for
grace, and when the time that you choose has come, to
visit me in mercy and set my heart aflame. I may not
burn with the great longing that those people feel who
are your especially devoted servants, yet through your
grace I at least long for the longing that flames in
them; and I pray and entreat you that I may be joined
with all those who love you with such a burning love,
and may be counted among their holy company.

[2] Luke 24.30-35

XV

The grace of devotion comes through humility and negation of self

THE VOICE OF THE BELOVED : If you desire the grace of devotion, you must seek it unceasingly, ask for it earnestly, and wait for it with patience and faith. When it comes you must receive it thankfully, preserve it humbly, use it thoughtfully; and leave with God the time and the way in which he will visit you from heaven, waiting till he comes.

When you feel little or no devotion in your heart, then is the time to humble yourself; but you must not be too dejected, nor unduly despondent, for God often gives in one brief moment what he has long been keeping from you, and sometimes grants at the end of your prayer the thing he held back at first. If grace were always given quickly and could be had for the asking, it would prove more than feeble mankind could endure. That is why you have to wait for the grace of devotion with a good hope and humble patience.

When devotion is not granted you or is even quietly removed, you must blame yourself and your sins. It is sometimes quite a small thing which hinders grace or hides it—if it can be called a small thing and not a serious one, when it keeps you from such a blessing. But whether it is small or great, once get rid of it and overcome it completely, and you will have the thing you asked for. As soon as you surrender yourself to God with all your heart, and no longer desire this or that at your own wish and whim, but let yourself depend entirely on him, you will know unity and peace. For nothing will then give you so much satisfaction and delight as doing the will of God.

If a man in all sincerity directs his whole intention up to God, if he empties himself of every undisciplined dislike or love for any created thing, then he will be fit to receive the gift of grace and will be worthy of the blessing of devotion. For God pours out his blessing into vessels he finds empty. It is when a man renounces all that is base, scorns the claims of self, and dies to all that self involves, that grace can come to him quickly and in abundance, and bear his heart unhindered to the heights.

Then that man's heart shall overflow with wonder and gratitude[1] at what he sees, because the might of God is with him, and he has entrusted himself to his power for ever. Such is the blessing that awaits a man[2] who makes God the whole quest of his heart,[3] and never sets his heart on lying tales.[4] When this sort of man receives the Holy Eucharist, he is found fit for the grace of union with God, because he is not thinking of his personal devotion and comfort, but above all devotion and comfort he is thinking of the glory and honour of God.

XVI

We should tell Christ of our difficulties and ask for his grace

THE VOICE OF THE DISCIPLE : Most gentle and loving Lord, I long to receive you now with devotion. You know my weakness and my need; you know the evils and the faults that hold me. You know how often I am

[1] Is. 60.5
[2] Ps. 127.4
[3] Ps. 118.2
[4] Ps. 23.4

burdened, tempted, troubled, defiled. I come to you for healing; I beg for help and comfort. I call on you, for you know all things and see all my secret being; you only can comfort me and bring me lasting help. You know what good things I have most need of, you know how poor I am in virtues. Here I stand before you, naked and destitute, begging you for grace, imploring you for mercy.

Feed me, for I come hungry to your door; melt my coldness with the fire of your love, and with the brightness of your presence make my darkness light. Turn all earthly things to bitterness for me; all that is difficult and hard to bear, turn into patience; all that is base and created, into scorning and forgetfulness. Lift up my heart to you in heaven, and do not send me away to wander on the earth. Make yourself my sole delight, from now on and for ever; for you are my only food and drink, my love and joy, my sweetness and all my good.

How I long for you to set my whole being aflame with your presence, to consume me and transmute me, to make me one spirit with yourself[1] through the grace of inward union, and the burning love that dissolves me in its heat. Do not let me go away from you barren and loveless, but deal with me mercifully, as you have so often and so wonderfully dealt with all your saints.

In your presence I may well lose myself and be wholly turned to flame; for you are a fire that burns for ever, never dying down, a love that purifies the heart and fills the mind with light.

[1] I Cor. 6.17

XVII

Concerning that burning love and eager longing to receive Christ

THE DISCIPLE : With deep devotion and fervent love, with all the affection and warmth of my heart, I long to receive you, Lord, as I communicate, no less than all those saints and devout people longed for you, who pleased you by the holiness of their lives and knew a burning devotion. O God, eternal love, my whole good, my endless blessedness, I want to receive you with the deepest longing and the most worthy reverence that any of the saints ever had or could have. I know I am not fit to have those feelings of devotion, yet I offer you all the love of my heart, just as if all those wonderful fires of longing could be concentrated in me alone. Whatever a loving soul can feel and desire, that I bring and offer you, with the deepest reverence and affection in my heart. I do not want to keep anything back for myself, but gladly and of my own free will I sacrifice to you myself and all I have.

O Lord my God, my Creator and Redeemer, I long to receive you today with affection and reverence, with praise and honour, with thanks, respect and love, with faith and hope and purity, just as your most holy Mother, the glorious Virgin Mary, longed for you and received you, when the angel brought her news of the mystery of the Incarnation, and she humbly and devoutly replied : *Behold the handmaid of the Lord; let it be unto me according to thy word.*[1] Your blessed herald, John the Baptist, the most excellent of the saints, rejoiced in your presence and leapt with the joy

[1] Luke 1.38

of the Holy Spirit while he was still in his mother's womb;[2] and later when he saw Jesus walking about among men, he humbled himself and with love and devotion said : ' *The bridegroom's friend who stands by and listens to him rejoices too, rejoices at hearing the bridegroom's voice.*'[3] In the same way, I long to be filled with a burning holy desire and to offer you myself wholeheartedly. For that reason, I present and offer to you the rejoicing of all hearts that are devout, their burning love, their ecstasies, their heavenly visions, their times of illumination from above. I offer them with all the virtues and all the praises that have been or shall be sung by every creature in heaven and on the earth, on my own behalf and on behalf of all those who have been commended to my prayers. May they all render you the praise they owe, and glorify you for ever.

O Lord my God, receive my prayer and my desire to praise you for ever and bless you endlessly, all of which I owe you for the immensity of your unutterable greatness. This I offer, and desire to offer every day, and every moment of every day. To offer thanks and praise along with me I invite and exhort by my prayers and longings all heavenly spirits and all your faithful people. Let all people praise you, all tribes and tongues, and let them with jubilation and burning love praise your holy name, as sweet as honey on the tongue. May all those who celebrate your exalted Sacrament with reverence and devotion, and receive it in complete faith, be granted grace and mercy, and may they prayerfully entreat you on behalf of me, a sinner. When they have experienced that longed-for devotion and the joy of union with you, as they come away comforted and wonderfully refreshed from the holy heavenly table, may they be so kind as to think of one so spiritually poor as me.

[2] Luke 1.44   [3] John 3.29

XVIII

Do not investigate the Sacrament to satisfy your curiosity, but follow Christ humbly, subordinating understanding to holy faith

THE VOICE OF THE BELOVED : You must beware of trying to fathom the mysteries of this Sacrament out of useless curiosity, unless you want to be drowned in a flood of doubt.

Search too high, and the brightness shall dazzle thee.[1] God can do more than man can understand. What is allowed you is a humble and reverent search for truth, in which a man is always prepared to learn, and eager to direct his steps according to the sound views of the Fathers. It is the simple approach that is blessed, one that avoids the thorny paths of debate, and marches along the firm smooth road of God's commands.

Many people have destroyed their devotion by trying to look into things too deep for them. It is faith that is expected of you and honest living, not profound understanding and deep knowledge of the mysteries of God. If you cannot grasp or understand things that are less than yourself, how will you take in greater ones? You must submit to God, and subordinate understanding to faith—then you will be given the light of knowledge in so far as you need it and it is good for you.

Some people are hard tempted as regards faith and the Sacrament, but it is not they who are to be blamed so much as the Enemy. Pay no attention to such attacks. Do not argue in your own mind, or try to answer the doubts the Devil hurls against you. Trust the

[1] Prov. 25.27

word of God, believe his saints and prophets, and you will put your wicked enemy to flight.

It is often very good for God's servant to endure this sort of thing. The Devil does not tempt the faithless and the wicked, for he has them in his power; but he tempts and harasses the devout and faithful in all the ways he can. You must press on with simple undoubting faith; approach the Sacrament with prayerful reverence, and calmly leave with God the all-powerful whatever you cannot understand.

God does not deceive you, but you will be deceived if you trust too much to yourself. God walks with simple people, and reveals himself to humble ones. It is to those who become like children that he gives understanding, and he enlarges the faculties of minds that are pure; but from those who are arrogant and inquisitive he keeps his grace concealed. Human understanding is weak and easily deceived, but true faith cannot be led astray.

Understanding and inquiry should follow faith, not precede and weaken it. In this holy and most excellent Sacrament, it is faith and love that are all-important, and they work in secret ways. God who is eternal, infinite, supremely mighty, does great and unfathomable things in heaven and in earth, and there is no understanding his wonderful works. If the works of God could easily be grasped by human understanding, they could not be called wonderful or too great for words.

SELECT BIBLIOGRAPHY

Of the numerous editions of the writings of Thomas à Kempis in Latin, the following may be mentioned as being comparatively recent:

Complete works: POHL, M. J., 8 vols., Freiburg, 1902-18

De Imitatione Christi: HIRSCHE, K., Berlin, 1874, 2nd edit., 1891 (text based on the 1441 autograph manuscript)

As far as translations are concerned, fresh English versions of *The Imitation of Christ* apart from the other works have been appearing at intervals ever since the fifteenth century. A list 'of the different original translations, adaptations and paraphrases' (thirty-three in number) which appeared up to 1900 may be found in:

COPINGER, W. A.: 'On the English Translations of the 'Imitatio Christi,' *Bibliographiana* No. 3, Manchester, 1900

The most distinguished of these versions were probably those of John Wesley (1735) and Bishop Challoner (1737), both of which have been frequently reprinted. The early English translations may be found in: Publications of the Early English Text Society, extra series 63 (London 1893), containing the Old English version (c. 1460), also Books 1-3 trans. by William Atkynson, D.D., Book 4 by Lady Margaret, mother of King Henry VII, Countess of Richmond and Derby (c. 1504).

Recent versions include:

SHERLEY-PRICE, L., Penguin Classics, 1952

MCCANN, ABBOT JUSTIN, London, 1954.

KNOX, RONALD, and OAKLEY, MICHAEL, Universe Books, London, 1959

The controversy over the authorship of the *Imitation* and the resulting interest in Thomas à Kempis have occasioned a vast number of books and articles on these subjects from Continental countries. Books in English are fewer in number, and as they were mostly products of the nineteenth century, they are not readily available today. The following may, however, be discovered in reference libraries :

CRUISE, SIR F. R., *Thomas à Kempis, notes of a visit to the scenes in which his life was spent*, London, 1887

An outline of the life of Thomas à Kempis, Dublin, 1907

KETTLEWELL, S., *The authorship of the ' Imitatio Christi'*, London, 1877

Thomas à Kempis and the Brothers of the Common Life, London, 1882

WHEATLEY, L. A., *The story of the ' Imitatio Christi'*, The Book-Lover's Library, London, 1891

To the same period belongs a facsimile of the 1441 manuscript :

The Imitation of Christ; being the autograph manuscript of Thomas à Kempis reproduced in facsimile, with an introduction by C. Ruelens, London, 1879

See also :

BARRON, D. G., *Jean Charlier de Gerson, the Author of the ' De Imitatione Christi'*, Edinburgh, 1936

For further information on the historical and religious background, see :

CLARK, JAMES M., *The great German mystics: Eckhart, Tauler and Suso*, Modern Language Studies, v, Oxford, 1949

HUIZINGA, J., *The Waning of the Middle Ages*, London, 1924 (Pelican Books 1955)

HYMA, A., *The Christian Renaissance, a history of the Devotio Moderna*, New York and London, 1925

JACOB, E. F., *Essays in the Conciliar Epoch*, ch. 7— 'The Brethren of the Common Life', Manchester University Publications, Historical Series 80, Manchester, 1943

JONES, RUFUS M., *Studies in Mystical Religion* (chs. 11-14), London, 1919

KNOWLES, DAVID, *The English Mystical Tradition*, London, 1961

SITWELL, DOM GERARD, *Medieval Spiritual Writers* (Faith and Fact Books : 40), London, 1961

The Oxford Dictionary of the Christian Church, Oxford, 1957 (various articles, with bibliographies, e.g. 'Thomas à Kempis'; 'Imitation of Christ'; 'Devotio Moderna'; 'Brethren of the Common Life'; 'Groote, Gert de'; 'Ruysbroeck, Jan van'; 'Florentius Radewyns'; 'Augustinian Canons'; 'Windesheim'.)

Also available in Fount Paperbacks

Erasmus of Christendom
R. H. BAINTON

'In this book, which carries lightly and easily the massive Erasmian scholarship of the last half-century, Erasmus comes to life. He speaks for himself, and, speaking, reveals himself.'

Hugh Trevor-Roper, Sunday Times

Calvin
FRANÇOIS WENDEL

'This is the best introduction to Calvin and his theology that has been written, and it is a work of scholarship which one salutes and admires.'

Professor Gordon Rupp

Bonhoeffer: An Illustrated Introduction
EBERHARD BETHGE

'. . . we have facts reviewed which were not generally known before. The number of portraits are really first class.'

Christian Herald

Gateway to God
SIMONE WEIL

'Simone . . . makes everything seem, at once, reassuringly recognizable and so luminous as to be heavenly . . . the great mysteries . . . are seen through a window of time in the perspective of eternity.'

Malcolm Muggeridge